TABLE OF CONTENTS

FOREWORD

I met Shiv in 2014, during a consulting job and we became fast friends. A little about me: Firstly, as the executive director of an NPO, I've chosen to remain anonymous in this foreword. As a technology consultant, I've spent my career analyzing hardware, software and network capabilities; troubleshooting issues, and developing innovative solutions for businesses to drive growth. As a stock trader, I've spent many years buying and selling stock.

Years ago, Shiv shared a story with me, one that dates back to the year 2000, also known as the "Dot-com Bubble Burst." *According to Investopedia, "The dotcom bubble burst when capital began to dry up. In the years preceding the bubble, record low interest rates, the adoption of the Internet, and interest in technology companies allowed capital to flow freely, especially to startup companies that had no track record of success."* Shiv had recently immigrated to the US and was in his first year of living here, when he was introduced to the US stock market for the very first time. I must say, this was probably not the best time, if not the worst, to get your feet wet with the stock market; the great technology bubble was at its peak.

Shiv possessed a technology background, primarily in programming and databases. He worked at an US-based IT consulting firm and was traveling from one client site to another for short or mid-term IT consulting engagements. One of his clients introduced him to Prasad, a colleague, and later a close confidante. One day, Prasad started to speak about the stock market and how his portfolio profits had risen 10X in the bull market of 1999. This caught Shiv's attention and his curiosity led him to learn more. Before long, Shiv took his first step, opened his first ever trading account with e-trade, and funded it with a decent 4-figures from his savings.

I should emphasize at this point that Shiv had absolutely zero knowledge of the stock market; he was a complete novice. Shiv quickly realized that simply funding the account would not be enough to grow his money by 10X, like Prasad did over a few years. Shiv decided to move fast and take action to build his portfolio. Shiv asked Prasad to let him in on some of his best performing 10X profit stocks. Prasad shared his "tools of the trade" with Shiv, not knowing what was running through Shiv's mind. Shiv got that list from Prasad and simply went ahead—and bought each of those stocks. That was Shiv's plan for jump starting his investment and building his portfolio. He had done absolutely zero research, nor did he possess any understanding of the stocks he bought (or the stock market in general).

Within a few months, the Dot-com Bubble Burst happened. Shiv watched his portfolio value drop by almost 50%, didn't take any action, and just kept hoping that the stocks he bought would bounce back someday; he was convinced he would also earn a 10X return in his investments, like Prasad did. I remember Shiv saying that when he looked at his portfolio a few months after the bubble burst, there was only $155 left. He mentioned that one of the stocks he had bought for $132 per share, became a penny stock worth nothing after the crash. At that time, Shiv was adamant that he would never step back into the stock market.

By my estimation, more than 90% of people who enter the stock market do so with limited or no knowledge at all; and Shiv's experience is a perfect example. Most end up falling into the trap of being influenced by big flashy profits that others are making—and attempt to imitate their success without taking time to build the foundation required (to know when the time is right). In 2008, Shiv was introduced to a financial advisor who became a close friend of his, while giving him financial advice for 10 years. That year, Shiv resumed investing in the market, but only with the help of this financial advisor and friend. Shiv continued to refrain from directly buying stocks until he passed the age of 40. His initial bad experience and fear of losing his hard-earned money, kept him from trying to learn the basics of the stock market.

Fast forward to 2016, Shiv met his stock market mentor, who goes by the name of Guru. He came into Shiv's life right around the time Shiv was struggling to achieve work-life balance. He was looking after his ailing mother at home, who was beginning to require more and more care, beyond what the homecare workers could provide. Shiv comes from a cultural background where the responsibility of taking care of your parents, falls on the son; since Shiv was the only son, he juggled that responsibility along with his day job.

Guru soon became a good friend, visiting Shiv's home frequently, and he even built a special bond with Shiv's mother. I know Shiv considers Guru a godsend during those times, when he needed a friend by his side to provide moral support. Shiv also quit his very demanding day job at this time and got into consulting, which was more flexible and allowed him to work from home so he could take care of his mother.

One day, Guru shared that he had been studying the stock market very deeply and had learned that it requires considerably basic analytical skills and more importantly, great discipline to make money. He said anyone who has discipline can make money by just unemotionally, mechanically following a few key trading strategies and rules. He further emphasized that anyone who can master self-discipline, these few key trading strategies and dedication, may have a better chance—and potentially earn a consistent stream of profits. After noticing that Shiv was one of the most disciplined and principled people he had ever come across (when it came to money management) Guru volunteered to teach Shiv the fundamentals of the stock market, as well as core strategies of day trading. Shiv was intrigued and he readily accepted the offer.

Over the course of several months, Guru and Shiv spent their weeknights going through the stock market and bouncing ideas back and forth. Before Shiv even realized it, within a couple of months and probably 4-5 sessions, he had made a profit of over $1,000 just by practicing small trades. Within the first year of learning from Guru, Shiv netted a profit of $9,000; in the second year, $16,000. This was all just by trading on and off, as time permitted, during the evenings or early mornings. Shiv continued to work at his day job, then, right around that time, the pandemic hit. He managed to juggle caring for his mother at home while doing his day job remotely. This gave him some time in the evenings, early mornings, and weekends for trading. Shiv started to spend time, with help from Guru, studying, experimenting, preparing, measuring, recalibrating, and most importantly, making money in the stock market.

After that, Shiv reached a point where he felt he knew it all and could almost predict how the market would behave the next day. He was earning six-figures in profits from the stock market and crypto market. Did you know that Shiv made a six-figure profit, before losing the same amount TWICE? I believe that it transpired due to a lack of discipline and I'm so glad he managed to bounce back from that nightmare. This is precisely why Shiv Verma is qualified to author this unique, relatable book full of invaluable dos and don'ts, that will help you master the art of trading! I urge you to adopt the priceless wisdom in here, allow it to increase your likelihood of becoming a better trader, who makes profitable trades, and hopefully become a Wall Street Surfer!

PREFACE

Life is short and your time is precious, let me save you months—maybe years—of headaches and heartache; by sharing my insights and teachable experiences with you. The objective of this book is to help you become a better student of trading, create disciplined trading habits, and reveal your trading potential. Most importantly, I'm here to endlessly remind you to follow precautions, minimize losses, and avoid financial loss from trading! If you gift this book to a teenager, young adult, or any human in your life, it could very well save them from financial devastation; think of the brownie points you'd earn then!

When conducting research for this book, I discovered that over 90% of people lose money in trading. I believe that if you learn from my mistakes, then you won't become a part of that sad statistic. I learned the hard way; I wish that I could have learned from the mistakes of others instead. I wish I had a book like this one, before I set foot into the stock market. However, there's one very notable book, called "Trading in the Zone" by the late Mark Douglas (available on www.paulatwebb.com and Amazon).

Use the lessons here, in Trading Rewired, to lay a strong foundation, plinth beam and slab, then, ensure that every aspect of your frame is concrete. After that, you may add on other books, which may serve as your insulation and waterproofing. Without a strong foundation, cracks will begin to appear on your walls and weaken your structure. Poor insulation and waterproofing means high energy bills, water damage, and mold that will gradually infiltrate your construction. Both are indispensable. I must congratulate you for being here. The fact that you're reading my book, means that your about to embark on a powerful journey—or, you haven't given up and are ready to give this another shot!

This book will walk you through, step by step; how I made mistakes commonly made by those who lose money trading.

During the bull market years, I was earning a return and profiting on most trades. According to IG.com, “Bulls are used to refer to an upward trending market, a cycle of growth.” Yes, you heard right! During extreme bull market conditions, one can frequently get lucky. However, the goal is not to pull off “beginner’s luck” but to become skilled and consistent. Funnily enough, my mentor, Guru used to caution me on such common mistakes, yet I made those mistakes again and again.

Let me be clear, trading is not gambling, never bet on Wall Street. Instead, be a consistent Wall Street surfer; consistent surfers can get lucky too, perhaps even more than those who bet blindly. Often, when consistent surfers are rewarded with big wins, people will say they got lucky. Well, in a way, they’re right, they got lucky as a result of the consistent hard work they put in!

Being undisciplined and obliviously riding a bull, I was about to learn a hard lesson. When the pandemic hit, the market crashed and a period of extreme market volatility began. This was a true test of my skills and quickly I realized my weaknesses. I also learned that some people lost fortunes trading in the stock market. Not only was the news constantly reporting human tragedies due to the pandemic, but also due to the stock market crash of 2020. I hope to help people become better aware of their trading skills and avoid these types of tragedies—brought on by the major market volatility.

Not going to lie, before 2017-2018, I was under the belief that trading requires extremely specialized financial, technical, and analytical skills. In other words, skills that would require one to have a master’s degree, at the very least. I stand here today, in 2022 and 2023, confidently declaring that above all, trading requires rock-solid discipline. While basic technical and analytical skills are good to have, they can be developed within a few weeks (or a couple of months at the most), if I’m being honest.

It's a harsh fact that more than 90% of the people who start trading will lose money. If you do a search on the web today, you will be surprised to find out the statistics around how miserably most traders fail. I use the word "fail," because most of them give up trying after starting off on the wrong foot. What do I mean by the wrong foot? Diving into trading head first, fantasizing about getting rich quick, that's a mistake. The sooner you ingrain this into your mind, the sooner I can stop sounding like a broken record! Mark my words, if you go in with this a false mindset, it's extremely unlikely that you'll become a winner on Wall Street.

Speaking of mindsets, I have generally been a pretty disciplined person all my life, this was the very reason that my mentor, Guru, willingly taught me everything he knew about the stock market. He told me that he didn't usually share his trading secrets so easily with others, because he mostly found that people weren't disciplined enough (and often ended up on the losing side). Guru showed confidence in me and regretfully, I not only disappointed him but also myself. It was shocking, how carried away I got while trading, despite my disciplined life.

My lecturing tone may test your patience at times; but patience in traders is worth a king's ransom. There was a time when my overconfidence and lack of patience caused me to think that I already knew it all. This reminds me of two quotes: One by Ralph Marston, "When you think you know it all, there's not much that you'll learn." Another by Stephen Hawking, "The greatest enemy of knowledge is not ignorance, it is the illusion of knowledge." This is why we should regularly pause and take inventory of our minds, to ensure that we remain humble, life-long students.

In his book, Mark Douglas rightfully said, "The goal of any trader is to turn profits on a regular basis, yet so few people ever really make consistent money as traders. What accounts for the small percentage of traders who are consistently successful? To me, the determining factor is psychological—the consistent winners think differently from everyone else." Here's something remarkably interesting: at one point, I realized that in my gut, over 80% of the time, I knew which direction the market would go in. Yet, I still managed to fail in my trades due to a lack of confidence in my disciplined approach. Some of the financial numbers shared in the book are more directional and estimated ballpark to the best of my memory. They are there to help portrait the true real story and the underlying message related to the risk of trading.

In order to be a successful trader, I needed to have confidence in my own trades and trust myself to make the right moves, without indecision. Instead, I constantly doubted myself and feared the erratic behavior of the market. This resulted in my failure to stick to my trading discipline. *According to FXTM, "discipline involves having and sticking to a trading plan. Create a schedule for your trading and know what signals will help to decide to enter or exit a trade. Ensure that you apply proper risk management by sticking to your stop loss and take profit orders."* Now, it's time to rewire everything you thought you knew about trading! Time to ride the waves of Wall Street, as pro surfers and not amateur gamblers!

IS THIS BOOK FOR YOU?

- Are you interested in becoming financially independent?
- Are you wondering how you can set yourself up for a successful life?
- Are you interested in learning about stock market trading?
- Are you part of the 90% who haven't had success at stock market trading?
- Are you curious about how to make extra money on the side through stock market trading?

This book will show you how to become a thriving trader, share my challenges and how I overcame them, tell you how I succeeded and failed miserably before bouncing back using discipline, and help you find parallels to your own story. I'm not a financial advisor or psychologist. I'm just a regular person—and if I could bounce back from that nightmare, you can too. I wrote this book so that it can reach other people like you and I, who could use some guidance to avoid the financial hell that I experienced.

If something comes too easily to you—without any effort—you'll likely take it for granted. Just like how Guru told me that it was his mistake for teaching me so nonchalantly and spoon-feeding me trading knowledge. Because of that, I didn't value it or take it seriously—but now I understand his perspective. Over the past year, I've earned it; dedicating myself, learning, mastering the skill with discipline, and putting in the time. The days of looking to Guru and copying every trade so I didn't have to think for myself—are over. Being a brainless copycat trader is not the way! Now, I spend quality time with Guru discussing broader strategies.

A HUMBLE APPEAL

You may have noticed that English is my second language, actually it's my fourth! Where I'm from, we have a national language, a mother tongue, and a native language, which makes English my fourth language. I may not be an expert in vocabulary, but I'd like to think that you're able to follow my English and appreciate the read. Also, shout out to my editor, Michelle Wiebe, for exceeding expectations and helping me shape my words into a more natural, conversational, expressive tone—so it's not "just another lifeless trading handbook."

Imagine sitting at a cozy café and enjoying a casual conversation with a friend. I'm that friend who's eager to share his experiences with you. This friend's genuine intention is to help you avoid the mistakes I made. I want you to learn from my mistakes and be a better trader and better person. So, if you find me ranting or repeating myself in the book—as an old friend does—just stick with me and I'll take good care of you. I can assure you that even if you read this book multiple times a year, it will only help you get further with a better perspective.

At least 35% of the profits generated from this book has been pledged as a donation towards helping the elderly and people with chronic diseases. Full confession though, as they say, charity begins at home; so, the first person I will help is my sister. She has been my life coach and mentor. I want to help her fulfill her dream of setting up shelters for seniors and people with disabilities experiencing homelessness.

So how can you help me with our cause? Well, you already have! You're reading or listening to this book! I'll receive a small royalty from whichever platform you purchased this book on—so THANK YOU! If you're wondering how else you can help, here are a few ideas:

- Leave a kind review for this book.
- Send your friends the link and tell them to purchase it!
- Buy a copy for a family member or friend as a gift.
- Share it on social media.
- Check out my other books based on true-story of my life at Rewired.guru "Books Page".
- Use my REFERRAL CODES from Rewired.guru when registering on any trading websites; occasionally there may be a surprise gift waiting for you too!
- Need reminders on how to become a successful trader? Check out our motivational posters at Rewired.guru "Product Page".
- Visit Rewired.guru for more ways to help my causes. Whatever you choose, just know that I appreciate you!

SETTING THE STAGE: BEFORE YOU BEGIN

This book is written for beginner and returning traders of all ages; anyone who is interested in understanding stock market trading discipline—and the psychology of earning decent money. The language in this book is simple enough for all learners to understand, regardless of whether you're 15 or 55. I've tried to keep it engaging by categorizing common traits and attributes of traders into different "trading identities".

The truth is, I've found myself going through all these phases over the past 6+ years. I've made a lot of money and also lost a lot of money; net-net I finally reached a point where I started to lose the money that I'd made from stock market trading. For simplicity, from this point forward, I'll refer to stock market trading as "trading" and to a stock market trader as "trader".

You'll learn the story of my almost 6 year learning phase, nearly reaching the point of quitting, how I shocked myself by behaving like a completely different person when trading, and taking one last shot at triaging (and remedying) my trading behaviors. In my day-to-day life, I'm a very calculated risk taker—or as some call it, "risk averse". Which is why experiencing such a wide variety of "trading identities" during those years was the biggest obstacle that held me back from success; success that I want you to achieve within a much shorter time frame.

It's evident to me now that my self-deprecating jokes about having "multiple personalities" was a coping mechanism—because it hurt me; it was the source of my failures (before I developed my trading discipline). Even my mentor admitted that he was shocked to see those sides of me brought out by trading. This journey has uncovered weaknesses that I was previously unaware of. I'm convinced that this is why they say 90% of beginner traders fail or give up. I truly believe that trading is a great additional income stream; but this goal is no different than going to the gym. Building your "trading muscles" will take time, practice, and patience. The good news is, once you've put in the time and work, you'll be able to do wonders with your newly developed strength; and you'll also have "muscle memory"!

My Trading Mantras:

"The more you practice (discipline), the luckier (more skilled) you become at profiting from trading."

"You can learn a lot from your various 'trading identities', as long as you don't allow any of them to hold you captive. There is a time for everything; times to be bettors, HODLers, overthinkers, non-starters, copycats, hopefuls, losers and surfers; until you become a master sailor!"

A quick PSA:

- Nothing is worth sacrificing your precious life for; your mental and physical health is more valuable than money. Believe me, money can be replaced. You are irreplaceable.
- There are no shortcuts—unless you win a jackpot or lottery; don't hold your breath.
- Analysis paralysis is a real thing; avoid overwhelming yourself with market information.
- The best way to combat FOMO (fear of missing out) and FUD (fear, uncertainty and doubt) is to put on your metaphorical noise canceling headphones!
- Accept that no one can accurately predict market trends 100% of the time.
- Without disciplined trading, you'll likely lose more than you win; with disciplined trading, you'll likely win more than you lose.

- Conduct a personal inventory with the help of this book; discover your strengths and weaknesses and pave your path towards becoming a Wall Street surfer!
- Know that there's always room for improvement; it ain't over until it's over.
- Avoid going on a rampage after encountering a loss; this can waste your time, energy or even more money.
- Focus on how well your trading system (strategies) works and less on how to "get rich".
- First, develop discipline (before a trading system). *Synonyms of "discipline" according to Oxford Languages: "control, order, routine, regimen, training, rules, strictness."*
- Never force your trades; you don't have an obligation to trade daily.
- This is a marathon, not a sprint; take baby steps.
- Never trade when in the wrong state of mind (i.e., feeling stressed).
- Money cannot buy true happiness; making a positive impact on the world (and the people in your life) is the currency of genuine fulfillment.

ACKNOWLEDGEMENT

This is the first book I wrote after my mother passed away; I lost her during the pandemic. She was always my inspiration, and as I started writing this book, so many memories of her came back to me. Any business, work, or trading that I ever started; I'd always discuss it with my mother. She was a school dropout, full of wisdom, and always had valuable advice for me.

When I started trading, I was so excited to share my profit insights with her. Almost always, she would say to me, "Make sure you take your profits. Don't indulge in risky trades. Make sure you don't trade with too much of your savings. Don't be greedy. Make sure you never take any loans or margins in order to trade. Don't spend too much time looking at screens." One time, I told her, "You don't have to repeat these words so often." She told me that it was her duty and I laughed out loud. Believe it or not, her constant reminders worked in my subconscious, ensuring I didn't make those mistakes. Sure enough, not long after my mother passed away, I made every trading mistake that my mother warned me against. This led me to learning the biggest financial lesson of my life.

I had no idea that my mother was such an integral part of my daily discipline. This reminds me of the saying, "Sometimes we don't realize what we have until it's gone." Today, I understand and respect my mother's daily words of wisdom to me. So, there's no way I could write this book without acknowledging my mother. Miss you mom—and thank you for everything!

Can't forget the other VIP in my life, my mentor, Guru, who taught me the ABCs of trading; I was extremely hesitant to set foot into the stock market. My hesitation was due to a lack of knowledge. Guru taught me the basics with such a dedication that I feel indebted to him.

I'd also like to take the opportunity to thank YOU! Yes, you—because you're reading this book, which helps me realize my vision to make a positive impact on the world. You can thank me later! I know you're laughing at this statement, so am I. Great, now we've had our ice breaker. Let's begin!

CHAPTER 0
IS TRADING FOR YOU?

"If you believe in yourself and have dedication and pride—and never quit—you will be a winner. The price of victory is high, but so are the rewards."

—Bear Bryant

We all begin each endeavor from the ground up. Did "Chapter 0" catch your attention? Good! Before we jump into this chapter, I must emphasize that none of the prior sections should be missed, this is the only way you'll be able to connect the dots. The introduction, leading up to this chapter, is equally important for you to absorb. Trust me. This is an extremely important chapter that will hopefully bring you some clarity regarding this book's contents.

Now, let's set the foundation, before we begin our climb up. If you feel discouraged while reading this chapter, yet continue to read further, you're off to a good start. Trading is not an easy game; can you hear me literally shouting this from the rooftops?!

Now, a disclaimer:

- If you're expecting this book to make you a millionaire overnight, think again, unless you have a magic wand hidden up your sleeve. You may assume that this book was simply written by another guy who got lucky trading, however, you may be surprised how much you can learn from this commoner. If your hope is to find valuable insights, put some key trading mistakes on your radar, and learn how to become better at trading (from this moment forth), then you've found the right book.
- If you believe this book will help identify your hidden weaknesses in trading, you're a quick study!

- If you have a highlighter in hand, ready to underline my tips on how to approach trading, we're going to get along just fine!

Alright, glad you've made it this far, after reading all the previous sections of this book. You're now ready to roll! Before we take off, a philosophically relevant message: "If you want to fly, you have to give up the things that weigh you down." —Toni Morrison. The same goes for trading, if you genuinely want to learn to be a successful trader, you're going to have to dig deep within yourself. Here are some things that make people prone to trading failures, again and again:

- They aren't willing to learn discipline.
- They don't have a battle plan.
- They have a hard time accepting losses.
- They're excessively fearful or doubtful.
- They think that with discipline and a battle plan, all trades will be winners—this is a myth.
- They're unwilling to commit the time required to succeed.
- They can't handle the stress of trading volatility and unpredictability.
- They're unable to handle the pressure of needing to make the right decision, every step of the way.
- They're too impulsive, impatient, love to gamble, or lack emotional regulation skills.
- They have difficulty moving on from their mistakes; by learning, growing, and adapting.
- They're just out there for the adrenaline rush, quick wins, and fun games.
- They simply want to get rich quickly, without realizing that most aren't lucky enough to "hit the jackpot."
- They're looking at trading as a detour to becoming a millionaire overnight or retire quickly.
- They have trouble with impulse control; can't resist temptation.

- They tend to fight, flight, or freeze.
- They just want to try it because they saw someone on social media say "they made millions doing this."
- They're entering with unrealistic expectations—or just hate their job.
- They're egoistic, hotheaded, lack common sense, or are just plain reckless.
- They're going through physical or emotional turmoil. If this is you, please take some time for yourself.
- They're into blame games and will find a way to blame the market for their poor trading decisions.

Now, let's pause and allow all of that to soak in for a moment, before we move on to the next chapter of new beginnings! Next, an important message: Once you're done reading this book, I genuinely hope you work towards implementing what you have learned here. Implementation is the key. Knowledge without action is not worth a dime (and will likely leave you in a state of analysis paralysis). Being proactive, taking practical steps towards improvement, consistently observing the results, and evaluating your progress is the key to success.

It's crucial that you understand the fundamental difference between knowing and doing. Doing is in the practice, it's in the action. This is what world class professional musicians, athletes, singers, or traders do. They practice day in and day out—and are consistent with their practice; observing, learning, and outperforming themselves each day. Mastery of a trading mind comes with constant practice and improving from applying your daily learnings. Self-discipline will pave the way to your goals!

Remember, after giving it a try, if you find out that trading isn't for you, that's perfectly fine. You'll benefit for a lifetime from the knowledge gained, thanks to this experience. Your newly acquired wisdom will become a valuable tool for future investments. However, if you don't try, you'll never know what you're capable of, just be mindful to prevent burnout. If you start to feel frustrated or overwhelmed, take a step back. This is a marathon, not a race!

My formula for lasting long on this journey: Trust the process and give it some time before you jump ship! Trading is a difficult skill to acquire, it calls for years of learning, trials and errors—but once you have these tools under your belt, you'll be well equipped for the journey. Stay focused, one step at a time, slow and steady wins the marathon. You're your only competition, no one else.

As you embark on this journey, it's absolutely paramount that you don't allow yourself to burn out; which often leaves traders at a high risk for massive losses, both financially and physically. Your physical wellbeing, your mental health, and your family should be treasured above all else! Life is fragile, friends. I've witnessed so many people, here one moment and gone the next. We must not take our time on Earth for granted. We have to cherish each day that we get to wake up, we can't throw away our privilege of being alive. This is an issue that is near and dear to my heart, thus, I really hope my words resonate with you.

CHAPTER 1
ROAD TO TRADING: THE BEGINNING

"Whether you think you can or you think you cannot—you are right."

—Henry Ford

Flashback to the year 2000: When the dot com bubble was at its peak; I got my first taste of the stock market. Before I could even acclimate to it, the dot com bubble burst. That was a big non-starter for me; you already learned this from the foreword. If you skipped the foreword or other sections prior to this chapter, I encourage you to go back and read it, as they all serve a purpose. This is the beginning of your test on patience and discipline, my friend! Each section above contains a piece of the puzzle that is of value and relevance. Trust me, I will not lead you astray!

Come to think of it, my awareness of trading probably started in my childhood. I have memories of stories about my great-grandfather, who was a master of commodity market trading; this was probably way back in the early 1900s (in the northern parts of India). On the other hand, my father wasn't really into the stock market, he was mostly interested in real estate and low-risk interest-based government-backed investments. Interestingly, the only company stock my father invested in went up a thousandfold in 25 years. Cashing out from that stock funded parts of my college tuition, when my father was no longer in this world.

I graduated with a Bachelor of Physics and completed my post-grad in Computer Sciences. However, I dropped out halfway through my master's program when I got an IT consulting opportunity in the U.S., right before the dot com bubble peaked. Back in India, I worked mostly as an independent software developer. One of the jobs I did, involved developing share transfer software. At the time, I had no idea that time shares still exchanged hands physically in the form of share transfer certificates.

Why bother mentioning my education when trading has nothing to do with these skills? Because I failed miserably after a few years of thinking I was successful, only to find out it was just a fluke. Because that is when I learned the importance of disciplined trading. What I'm trying to say is, you don't need to learn sophisticated programming, financial management, etc. Anyone with self-discipline can build the skills required within a few weeks to a few months. Nowadays, even 11-year-old kids are trading. In Japan, a taxi driver became a billionaire trading stocks!

Trading vs. Investing:

Trading: Different from investing; successful traders will naturally and gradually become good investors. It's simple; profits you make in trading should be invested into consistent income and growth. Trading requires more basic technical analysis with a short-term focus. Trading (short-term focus) can vary from minutes to hours with an immediate outcome of profit or loss. Rarely would it go on for multiple days or weeks; also known as swing trading. *Jesse Livermore, born in Massachusetts in 1877, began his trading career at the young age of 15. The first share he purchased earned a profit of $3.12 from $5, after teaching himself the art of trends. He also earned huge profits, before losing it all, going through two huge crises and then recovering from it all. He did all this through sticking to his own set of rules, leading him to be nicknamed the "The Great Bear of Wall Street."*

Investing: Requires much more understanding of the underlying fundamentals with a long-term focus. Investing (long-term focus) usually takes place over multiple years; sometimes even decades. Warren Buffett, who needs no introduction, is a great example of an extremely successful investor—who made his fortune by consistently relying on the time-tested rules of value investing.

Back to the Beginning:

In early to mid-2016, due to personal commitments on the home front, I decided to quit my highly demanding day job. My mother's health required constant attention. Juggling work and home duties was becoming incredibly challenging, while my own health was deteriorating. I managed a smooth exit with my manager, first by switching to part-time consulting and advisory roles, then within a couple of months—I was free. During this transition, I started to get concerned about what I should do next (that would allow me more flexibility); leaving me with time to care for my mother and time for myself.

One evening, out of the blue, Guru came over to my house, asking how my mother was doing. I had met Guru only a year before this visit; we'd built a good working relationship. To my surprise, Guru mentioned his trading skills, how he was making a decent profit trading, and that it could potentially generate a couple thousand dollars per month, as an additional income stream. To be honest, I was skeptical. I had already gotten a taste of the stock market and it was unpleasant, to say the least.

Guru thought that I might have even more success trading because of my low-risk, disciplined nature, which he had observed. (Of course, there's no way to know what kind of trader someone will be; everyone's different). Not only did he suggest that I consider learning, he even volunteered to teach me so I could get a jump start. Guru's generous offer was a godsend during those tough times. To date, I still thank the Universe for sending me such a great friend and mentor—as an answer to my dilemma (of what I should do next). That day, before Guru left my place, he assigned me some homework: "Open a trading account with TD Ameritrade."

A few days later, Guru returned; he spent nearly 3 hours educating me on the ABCs of stock market trading. I must say, that was an eye-opening 3 hours. He took a very systematic approach, teaching me the basics of trading. He introduced a computer software (for trading) to me, called "thinkorswim", you may have heard of it already. This was the first time I saw stock charts and learned some trading terms like "candle sticks, exponential moving average, relative strength index," etc. All jargon related to technical analysis. Guru said, "One only requires a handful of technical analysis understanding to gradually start learning about trading." He also pointed out that practice and discipline were essential ingredients in his recipe for success. I was confident I'd have no issues with that. Sadly, I was wrong.

Over the next several weeks, Guru continued to come over for a couple of hours each time. He instructed me like a teacher does for their student—and even conducted small tests to evaluate my understanding. I began to feel more confident in my knowledge; and then, I had a moment of regret. As I witnessed millions of dollars changing hands in the market within minutes and seconds, I regretted missing out on all of this action for nearly 20 years! This menacing mentality was the beginning of my subconscious greed to get rich quick! This attitude is a big no-no in trading; instead, measure your progress based on whether your trading strategies are working (consistently) or not—and whether you're profiting (consistently) or not.

Guru asked me to not start trading with real money but rather spend the first few weeks using a "Paper Trading" feature. *According to Investopedia, "A paper trade is a simulated trade that allows an investor to practice buying and selling without risking real money."* Guru also recommended a few YouTube videos and a couple of books; he said that should be more than enough for me to start with a few key trading strategies. Guru emphasized his hope that I'd be disciplined and not rush the process without proper practice. I smiled and confidently told him,

"Don't worry, I'm a very careful person, who always prefers the low-risk route."

My Trading Mantras:

"Remember, trends are your friends!" —Guru

"In a sense, technical analysis allows you to get into the mind of the market, to anticipate what's likely to happen next, based on the kind of patterns the market generated at some previous moment." —Mark Douglas

Hope was sprouting within me. Without a day job, I began to spend a lot more time watching the market, started to see how things flow, and noticed a few strategies. As I watched these charts, I learned that there were repeatable patterns that happened hour after hour, day after day, week after week, month after month—you get the picture! The trick is to align these patterns with your trading strategy. Before entering any trade, always ask yourself the following questions:

- Price per share: When should I enter in a trade?
- Realistic profit taking: At what levels should I take profits and exit my position?
- Acceptable loss levels: At what point should I exit a trade cutting the losses?
- Total cost of trade position: How much am I going to put into this trade?

This book is not here to teach you a bunch of advanced trading strategies or complicated instruments. I'm here to help you develop the disciplined mindset of a successful trader. Later in this book, I will touch on some aspects of key trading strategies.

Guru regularly checked-in with me over the next couple of months; we started brainstorming together. Convinced I could read the market's mind, I started to feel like I'd soon make millions. So, for no good reason, I decided to skip the paper trading practice and jumped straight into live trading (with my real money). This was a big mistake! Why did I do that, you ask? Well, I'd told myself, "I've watched the market enough, I'll mostly make profitable trades. I don't want to miss out on all this action doing paper trading." This is the voice of greed, my friends. Consider yourselves warned. BEWARE!

Thankfully, the conservative, low-risk me was still in there somewhere, along with my mother's words of wisdom, "don't risk your hard-earned money." So, my first trade was 10 positions of Amazon stock, priced around $1050 per share (before 1-20 stock split). I exited with roughly $100 in profits. HE SHOOTS! HE SCORES!!! Careful with my first earnings from day trading, I didn't go beyond 10 stocks—and always stuck to Amazon stock trading. That's when the joke that "I now work with Amazon" was born.

So, let's briefly recap how I got to this point:

- Around 40 hours of total training time with Guru over 4-6 weeks.
- Around 80 hours watching the market over 6-8 weeks.
- Around 20 hours of general market discussions with Guru over 6-8 weeks.
- Around 20 hours of watching YouTube videos recommended by Guru.

Wow! Within 160 hours of learning about trading, I felt like I was already at an intermediate stage of knowledge. Even after making almost six figures in profits, I was blissfully ignorant about what was going on, unaware of the fluke I was sitting on. It took a six-figure loss for me to realize that it was all a sheer fluke. People spend YEARS studying medicine, business, science, finance, and so on. After YEARS of attending lectures and lab sessions, reading and researching, writing papers, and studying for tests—they finally receive their degree (just like I did). Yet there I was, naive Shiv, roughly 160 hours of learning later, feeling like I'd mastered stock market trading. I wish I was kidding.

The missing ingredient was PRACTICE—and a lot of it! I skipped practicing my mental visualization techniques. I skipped putting in the time watching, learning, and creating my trading discipline; completely disregarding Guru's cautionary advice. Imagine showing up to compete in a soccer game, after 160 hours of WATCHING other people soccer, without training and preparing first. Yeah, bad idea.

Tell me, what sets pro athletes apart from amateur athletes? Yup, they stick to their daily routine and train every day—rain or shine. Louis Armstrong once said, "If I don't practice for a day, I know it. If I don't practice for two days, the critics know it. And if I don't practice for three days, the public knows it." So, you're not required to go through years of tertiary education in order to learn trading strategies based on technical analysis, it calls for dedication and commitment. Calvin Coolidge once said, "Knowledge comes, but wisdom lingers. It may not be difficult to store up in the mind a vast quantity of facts within a comparatively short time, but the ability to form judgments, requires the severe discipline of hard work and the tempering heat of experience and maturity." Unfortunately, I overlooked these key aspects in the heat of wanting to make quick money!

You may feel like I'm kind of ranting—but remember, this is what real friends do when they want to make sure you learn from their mistakes! Ok? Trust me! So, what did this super awesome friend of yours learn from his first experiences with the stock market? Read on!

FAQ:

Q: How much time did I spend watching the market charts?
A: An average of 4 hours per day.

Q: What times of the day did I watch market charts?
A: 8:30AM-10:30AM, 12:30PM-1:30PM, and 3:30PM-5:00PM. (Mind you, this was during my leave of absence; I admit this is a bit much)

Q: How many stocks did I watch?
A: 4; Apple, Amazon, Google, and Microsoft.

Q: How many charts did I have on my screen?
A: Just 1 chart and 1 watchlist.

Q: How many screens did I have?
A: One 17-inch laptop screen.

Q: What other activities did I do outside of this time?
A: After leaving my day job to care for my mother, I spent all my free time keeping her company, preparing meals for her, taking her to doctors' appointments, and running errands with/for her.

Q: How many trades did I do per week?
A: Roughly 10-15 trades per week.

Q: Did I keep any trade positions open overnight?
A: No.

Q: What was my usual position size?
A: I mostly traded Amazon or Google with ten stocks.

Q: What was my entry strategy?
A: Green candle closing above the exponential moving average (EMA-9). This was one of the simplest strategies I focused on as I was learning. *According to Stock Market Eye, "A green candlestick means that the opening price on that day was lower than the closing price that day (i.e., the price moved up during the day)."*

Q: Did I stick to my entry strategy?
A: For the most part, yes.

Q: What was my profit-taking mindset?
A: Roughly 1% upward move in price of stock. While having a strategy is essential for profit taking, I overlooked two foundational concepts called "support and resistance". *According to Investors Underground, "Charts visualize support and resistance levels. These are price levels that consistently reject attempts to exceed above (resistance) or below (support). Supports are a price level that the stock will not fall below. Resistance is a price level that the stock can't seem to rise above. The longer these levels hold, the more they become stabilized for an eventual breakout or breakdown. Breakouts form when the resistance is finally surpassed as buyers come in off the fence and short sellers buy to cover their shares. A breakdown form when the support level finally cracks as sellers panic to unload their positions and short sellers try to add to their positions in often on a spike in volume."*

Q: What was my strategy for cutting losses?
A: When I'd spot a $20 loss, I'd exit the position. In hindsight, this wasn't really the correct strategy; it was more emotional than technical.

Q: How many trading accounts did I have?
A: One with TD Ameritrade enabled for Day Trading. FYI, a certain balance must be maintained in your brokerage account to become eligible for day trading (this varies between brokerage firms). Also, my E-Trade brokerage account was still open—with a microscopic amount of money (from that catastrophe of mine back in the year 2000).

Q: What was my net profit/loss from day trading by the end of that year?
A: Approximately $2,500 (after 2 months of trading).

Q: How many days a month did I trade?
A: Roughly 16-18 days per month.

Q: What was the general state of my emotions?
A: Initially, I was like a kid with a new toy—happy and excited. This toy made me feel like it would magically mint money. (Full disclosure: I did experience some long-term effects from the stress of my mother, my sister, and my own health challenges. Don't forget, my family's hard times had me quitting my day job; with 6-8 months' worth of savings and an emergency fund.)

Q: How would I rank this trading strategy on a scale of 1-10?
A: Maybe 5 out of 10. The probability of success was higher because of the bullish trend. However, this is not a reliable, sustainable strategy.

Q: How would I rate my discipline on a scale of 1-10?
A: Probably 10 out of 10. I don't remember a single trade where I lost more than $20. I'm not kidding! Remember, cautious, risk-averse guy over here, always on guard. That nightmare in the year 2000 really kept me on my toes!

POP QUIZ:

Q: What year was this?
A: 2017 (well, only the last quarter of 2017 as I was still a newbie).

CHAPTER 2
ALONG CAME CRYPTO: THE LISTENER & LEARNER

"I remind myself every morning: Nothing I say this day will teach me anything. So, if I am going to learn, I must do it by listening."

—Larry King

At the end of 2018, I also got a taste of the emerging crypto market. Being in "learner mode", I was listening to everything related to trading. Guru briefly mentioned that trading can also be done in the crypto market. He pointed out one particular detail about crypto—you can trade 24-7-365. That sounded intriguing to me, I thought, "Even with a day job, I can still trade crypto in the evenings and weekends." However, crypto turned out to be a distraction from my niche. A word of advice: don't fall for hype, keep your eye on the ball.

Focus and discipline plays a huge role in stock market trading, regardless of your geological location, which is why it's endlessly mentioned in this book. There's beauty in focusing on one thing at a time. According to a study published in the European Journal of Social Psychology in 2010, the time it took 96 participants to reach 95% of automaticity ranged from 18 to 254 days. *According to the Psychology Dictionary, "Automaticity refers to an action that is so well practiced that it does not require conscious effort to carry it out."* So, let's focus on mastering one thing at a time—once you're well versed in disciplined stock trading, you may advance to trading options, FOREX, futures, and crypto. Like crypto, options were a distraction and delayed my progress. They're good for making decent money once you're more experienced and have accumulated some profits.

As I banked profits from trading in 2017, while learning, I was excited for what this year (2018) had in store for me. I continued to learn from Guru, as he generously shared his wisdom with me. There were times where I'd spend hours listening to his ideas and newfound knowledge. To learn more about the market, I even subscribed to a bunch of free trial services (discord groups, WhatsApp groups, Twitter, Reddit, etc.) which honestly was just TMI and not super helpful. By the way, TMI means "too much information", that's what the cool kids say.

Guru recommended me to practice more (trading), he never liked the way I started off trading with real money. Not only did he feel that my conservative demeanor was preventing me from opening positions with a quantity of 100 or more, but he also reviewed my trades and informed me that I was profiting by sheer fluke. Guru said I was skipping crucial steps of trading discipline and gave me the following feedback:

- I didn't take advantage of paper trading; missing out on the opportunity to practice trading with virtual money.
- Instead, I started with real money, which allowed my emotions to take the reins while my focus took a back seat.
- My profit-taking strategy was unreliable.
- My stop-loss strategy was unsound. *According to Corporate Finance Institute, "Stop-loss is a tool used by traders and investors to limit losses and reduce risk exposure."*
- My simple entry strategy was adequate for a beginner.
- My approach to limit the number of stocks to focus on was sensible.
- My selection of stocks were reasonable, as they were the lowest-risk stocks to day trade.

As you can see, Guru identified barriers that were standing in the way of my growth. He continually emphasized that I'd be better off switching to paper trading to train myself and gain confidence first. I acknowledged everything he said and decided to work towards correcting my errors. It only lasted a few days; following Guru's recommendation and paper trading. Every trade

I made was profitable because I followed the discipline strategies—but my mind was still not on board.

Soon, good old FOMO kicked in and I began to hyper-fixate on those profits that I could have banked if I'd done live trading. This was the beginning of desperation and suppressed frustration. All I could think about were the millions of dollars being exchanged every few seconds in the market. I didn't want to miss out anymore, so I switched back to live trading.

This time around, my strategy had improved—after only a few days of practice (in combination with the kind of discipline mentioned in chapter one) and I resumed primarily live trading Amazon stocks and sometimes Google stocks. Initially, I focused on the first hour of the market as my trading time. I made a few good trades with Amazon stocks and within a week, I cashed out roughly $500 in profits.

Numbers started to run through my mind, telling me that this would only make me around $2000 per month. This was not enough to meet my needs and with no day job, I started to feel the pressure, it was a race against the clock. Day trading was starting to look like an unreliable source of income, as I realized that it wasn't a shortcut to financial freedom. I needed to save up some capital first, before returning to this; this is when it became clear to me that this is a marathon—not a race.

Around mid-February, I started to explore job opportunities in parallel, as things at home for my mother improved—and I'd been without a job or consistent income for almost 4 months. The original plan was 6 months off, so I was running out of time. I started looking for a flexible job that allowed me to take care of my mother at home. This time, I was mindful of avoiding jobs that would demand day and night support. My last job was extremely demanding, taking up over 12 hours of my day. That kind of job just wasn't sustainable anymore, with my health and family commitments.

Thankfully, a friend recommended that I reach out to a colleague from a past job and said they might have something that matched my needs. After a few meetings and interviews, I was offered a consulting contract. Having a day job with a consistent income again was a huge relief. To this day, I'm still so thankful for this former colleague and this hiring manager for the opportunity. It took me a few months of dedicated hard work to get me up to speed in the new environment.

Luckily, my manager was one of the best humans I've ever met, especially with me only being a contractor at the time. I was very open when sharing my family situation with him, so he saw my dedication to work and accommodated my need for flexible hours. His kindness allowed me to continue caring for my mother and sister, both of whom were suffering from their chronic conditions.

You may feel like I've veered off course. However, my intentions to share details about my personal life with you are: (1) I want you to know me as a person, not just "some trader", perhaps there's something in my life that'll resonate with you. (2) Possessing strategies and knowledge of the market are not the only ingredients for success in trading. In the past, I still failed, despite having all the trading tools and technical skills. The missing ingredient was habit formation.

Check out this cool fact I learned from Positive Psychology, "Active habits are those we develop by repeated intention and effort, crystallizing as skills we perform with little or no thought. A gymnast practices walking, jumping, and flipping on a narrow beam until she can do all these maneuvers smoothly without falling." Ok… so what am I getting at? Hold on, there's more, listen to this, "The scientific perspective on habit formation is exemplified today by neuroscience research. This research has highlighted crucial brain pathways involved in forming habits. As you practice a skill, it becomes a habit, something you can do easily and automatically." There it is—automatically, this is where the magic happens, friends. Once your brain takes all those lessons learned and saves them into your "stored habits", they will become automatic.

This "automatic" ability will give you the power to execute tasks in accordance with your SOP. *According to Tech Target: "A standard operating procedure is a set of instructions that describe the step-by-step process to properly perform a routine activity. SOPs provide the policies, processes and standards needed for the organization to succeed. They can benefit a business by reducing errors, increasing efficiencies and profitability, creating a safe work environment and producing guidelines for how to resolve issues and overcome obstacles."* Wow, that's good. This is what I want for you, friend, to be consistent, unemotional, and in compliance with your SOP. Not only will habit formation rewire your trading system, but it'll also lead you to a healthier and more positive life! I don't know about you but that sounds pretty awesome to me!

As we wrap up this chapter, let's touch on some highlights:

- My thirst for knowledge had me starting 2018 with a bang, diligently learning and listening, not just from Guru but also the market.
- The additional trading account I'd opened for commission free trading. At that time, TD Ameritrade was charging me up to $6 per trade, which I felt was an unnecessary expense. After doing the math, I also discovered that I was paying over $150 in commissions for my trades in 2017, profits I could have kept for myself. $150 may not seem like much but it all adds up. Now, most platforms offer free trading, so don't be like me and give your bread away!
- I acclimated: I knew that with the new day job, I wouldn't be able to trade during regular stock market hours. So, I used my newly acquired skills to explore pre-market and post-market hours. Some people say that there's not much action during these hours—or can even be quite volatile at times. However, I believe that it doesn't matter. If you

follow your discipline, you can ride any market wave, any time of the day.

- I continued to stay focused on trading Amazon and Google stocks. 80% of my trades were favorable; which is more than the average trader expects. Even if you have a 50% success rate (following a trading discipline of say 2:1 profit to loss ratio), you'll still profit from 50% of trades.
  → For example: You buy 100 stocks for $10 each; this is your entry point.
  → Situation A: The trend is in your favor—so you sell the stock (at a predetermined level for a price of $10.50), this is your profit-taking. Now, each time you take a profit, you make $50. So, 50% success rate out of 100 trades = 50 trades. $50x50 = $2500 profit.
  → Situation B: The trend is not in your favor—so you sell the stock (at a predetermined level of $9.75), this is how you cut your losses. Now, each time you cut a loss; you lose $25. So, if you had 50 trades that were lost, then $25x50 = $1125 loss.
  Your net-net profit will be: $1125.

POP QUIZ:

Q: What year was this?
A: 2018 (Jan, Feb, Mar).

CHAPTER 3
NAVIGATING THE AMAZON RAINFOREST: EAGLE EYES

"I made my first album, and it was not a fluke because now I am on my 16th."

—Bonnie Raitt

After my day job started, it became harder and harder to even trade during the early mornings and late nights. I was left with limited time and energy between work and taking care of things at home; this did not come as a surprise to me. Gradually, I adapted, and started to make time on weekends to stay informed on the market. I knew that if I lost touch with it, I'd have to retrain myself after coming back. John Flanagan (famous Australian fantasy author) once said, "Don't practice until you get it right, practice until you never get it wrong." We must be lifelong learners, dedicated to consistent practice and improvement. Your passion for growth will serve as a driving force to level up, again and again.

My goal was to achieve financial freedom in the next couple of years, through trading, so I remained patient, focused, and disciplined. Firstly, I prioritized work and home. Then, any residual time went towards trading and keeping up to speed with the market. This may sound like a funny approach to trading—but in 2018, I only traded when I was in a positive mindset, no disruptions. That's when these reminders below were born.

My Trading Mantras:

"Only trade after I've completed work and home duties."

"Only trade when I feel rested and clearheaded."

"Only trade when I have a positive mindset, i.e. relaxed and happy."

"Only trade when I feel confident about my decisions."

"Only trade when it feels right; not forced out of obligation."

Another personal mantra of mine at the time was, "Make sure Mom is comfortable and relaxed, either busy watching her TV shows or fast asleep." She had gotten used to seeing me around all the time for almost six months, during my leave of absence from work. I felt guilty that she wasn't seeing as much of me, since I started my new day job. Thankfully, I still managed to find time in the evening to look at the market. PSA: When in doubt, always choose your family first, otherwise you'll just be trading absentmindedly; a common cause of screw-ups.

How did I manage to find time to trade, you ask? Well, sharing is caring so, here you go:

- If you can't find the time, then make the time. Evaluate your priorities and make a plan.
- To be a successful trader, all you need is an hour here and there—and stick to your trading discipline.
- Take control of your emotions, don't let them control you. *As Believe Perform says, "Regulating emotion is not easy and is something that should be practiced consistently. Common strategies to regulate emotion include setting goals, mindfulness, deep breathing, meditation, positive self-talk, listening to music and reflective practice."*
- Remember the automatic habits I mentioned earlier? This is when they'll come in handy for you.

There will be more on emotional regulation and forming automatic habits in the coming chapters. There's no shortcut, however, the good news is that it's not rocket science! In fact, it's very doable! A perfect Steve Jobs quote to insert here: "Simple can be harder than complex: You have to work hard to get your thinking clean to make it simple. But it's worth it in the end because once you get there, you can move mountains." Drill this into your brain, my friend.

So, my winning streak trading Amazon stocks continued; I stuck to my trading wisdom religiously. My mother always kept me in check with her wisdom, reminding me not to be greedy. If my memory serves me right, I was nearing $8,000 in profits at this time, 90% of that profit came from trading Amazon stock. My trading discipline was explained in earlier chapters, however, in order to avoid your brain from becoming desensitized to me repeatedly mentioning "trading discipline", let's refresh your memory. Here is a review with some added insights:

- 90% of the time, I only traded Amazon stocks.
- My entry was always to prioritize a "strong green candlestick"—when the close is higher than the open (along with ensuring that the green candle closed above the exponential moving average EMA 9)—indicating a strong buying pressure. *Investors Underground says, "Every candlestick tells a story of the buyers and sellers, supply and demand, fear and greed. It is important to keep in mind that most candle patterns need confirmation based on the context of the preceding candles and proceeding candle. Many newbies make the common mistake of spotting a single candle formation without taking the context into consideration."* Pro tip: EMA stands for Exponential Moving Average; WMA stands for Weighted Moving Average. *According to Quantified Strategies, "The 9-period EMA being above the 30-period WMA indicates an up-trending market, while the 9 EMA being below the 30 WMA indicates a down-trending market."*
- My trading time varied, depending on my availability during pre-market, post-market, and regular market hours. However, the folks at Investopedia say that the U.S./London markets overlap (8AM to noon EST) , has the

heaviest volume of trading and is best for trading opportunities.

- Newly acquired knowledge: I should keep a close eye on trading volumes. What do I mean, you ask? Well, regularly monitoring stock volume is an effective way to improve the timing of your entries and exits. An abnormal volume informs you of strong action, which is important information for your trading strategies.
- Another lesson learned: if you go for market orders (instead of limit orders) when trading off peak hours, you risk more price differences. *More info from TheStreet.com: "A market order offers the benefit of immediate purchase, though the investor is likely to pay a higher price. If the investor wants to use a limit order, he or she will set a cap on the highest price they are willing to pay for a share and indicate when the limit order will expire. In order for limit orders to execute, the market price must fall to the limit order price."*
- My stock size increased from 10 to 25.
- I took profits on the first resistance level above my entry. At times, I'd split selling 15 on the first resistance and if I spotted an uptrend, I'd hold the remaining 10 to exit once it reached the next resistance. *According to Investopedia, "Resistance occurs where an uptrend is expected to pause temporarily, due to a concentration of supply."*
- I cut losses on the first support level below my entry and never took chances with split-selling when cutting losses. *According to Investopedia, "Support occurs where a downtrend is expected to pause due to a concentration of demand."*
- After completing each trade, regardless of profit or loss, I'd spend time observing the market for a bit—to prepare myself for trading the next day (determining possible trends, support levels, and resistance levels).

- Also noteworthy: I experimented with trading in 1, 2, 3, 5, 10, 15, and 30-minute intervals. After some trial runs, I concluded that a 15-minute interval was my comfort zone. With 1, 2 or 3-minute intervals, I felt flustered by the market's fluctuations in such a short duration. On top of that, my mind could not process the market within those time frames effectively, whereas the 15-minute interval increased my success rates (in combination with technical analysis and sticking to my trading discipline listed above).
- I only traded on the days that I felt grounded. *Lakefront Psychology explains, "Being grounded refers to a feeling of being stable, at ease, and consciously present. When we feel grounded, we are able to accept and let go of the momentary tough moments throughout the day and are not easily influenced by other ideas or feelings. You feel more at peace with your authentic self."*
- Just like learning a new language, developing a trading plan and building your trading discipline will take time—and daily practice. Eventually, you'll be speaking this language fluently!

Looking back, I don't recall any of my Amazon stocks flopping; any losses occurred with other stocks. Whenever I had time, I'd experiment with another stock (using both similar and different strategies). Not going to lie, 80% of the time I strayed from my trading system, I had to cut losses. If you ever find yourself in that position, just remember the popular saying on Wall Street, "Cut your losses short and let your winners run!" Haha!

To be honest, I was probably looking at Amazon stock for at least 30 minutes, 3 to 4 days a week. Seriously, I began to see ocean waves in the charts and predict how high the wave would go, how low it would fall, and even how big of a splash it would generate. I couldn't help but wish that I had a lot more money to multiply, via riding those waves, but I reined in my emotions and gave myself a pep talk, reminding myself of the importance of my trading discipline and the automatic habits that I'd worked so hard to form. These pep talks kept me in check, I even had post-it notes along the entrance of my home office.

Within the first five months, I banked over $12,000 in profits. At this rate, it seemed like I could easily make $25,000 on the side, from trading (in 2018). I hope this section caught your attention. Remember, trend is your friend. Most importantly, knowing and identifying the market trend in a timely fashion is awesomesauce!

CHAPTER 4
MUCH OF A MUCHNESS: SURFERS vs. TRADERS

"Traders and surfers both must deal with feelings of missing out on the small ones, until the big one comes along. They also must deal with feelings of staying with the big one."

—Ed Seykota

The previous chapter clearly set the tone around success associated with the discipline it took for me to trade Amazon stocks. This discipline is the key. Have you ever watched surfers do their thing? I also call them "wave riders". There are countless videos of amazing surfers all over the world. Check them out, in your free time, if you're not familiar with their craft.

This chapter is longer than others. Get rid of all your distractions because what I'm about to share is the crème de la crème, my friends. If you grasp this and work towards mastering it, you'll have a higher chance of not only becoming a stock market baller but also a life baller!

Let's discuss the qualities of successful wave surfers vs. stock market surfers. I'm sure you're aware that there are many amateur surfers all over the world, yet very few achieve excellence like the pros. This holds good in any professional field—sports or otherwise. I could have picked any sport, but using surfing as an analogy for trading is truly—*chef's kiss*. Surfers ride the ocean waves; traders ride the market waves. Both of which need to master the art of analyzing, identifying, and understanding their respective waves.

Excelling at any art is a combined effort of body and mind. Achieving success is a path made of discipline, routine practice, dedication, and overcoming your fears. If you can conquer these, luck follows. That's what makes both a brilliant surfer and a brilliant trader. Also, surfing may seem like a solitary sport, as does trading.

Surfing requires technical excellence, so performance is critical. To be good at surfing, it requires investing one's time to improve their moves and overcome both physical and psychological limitations. Pro surfers are required to stay on top by training consistently and remembering that there's always room for improvement. All of the above sounds just like trading, doesn't it? Surfing requires a healthy lifestyle; a well-fed, well-rested, strengthened, and cared for body and mind is the foundation for your quality performance. These are all applicable to trading as well. That's right, mental health is health.

If you're not familiar with meditation or mindfulness, I highly recommend that you become acquainted with the practice now. The fastest way to end mental health stigma is for us all to train and strengthen our minds the same way the entire world promotes training and strengthening our bodies (for physical health). I challenge you to start every single trading day with at least 20 minutes of mindfulness or meditation and at least 20 minutes of exercise, then, notice the benefits.

Why am I such a huge advocate for the practice of mindfulness? Some of the benefits of meditation that neuroscientists have found, according to Healthline:

1. Reduce stress
2. Lessen anxiety
3. Improve self-image
4. Boost positivity and mood
5. Enhance self-awareness
6. Lengthen attention span
7. Generate kindness
8. Improve sleep

9. Lessen pain
10. Decrease blood pressure
11. May reduce age-related memory loss
12. May help fight addiction

Surfers need to be resilient and so do traders. The ocean sometimes demands surfers to not just be brave but also resilient. There will be ups and downs but with focus, revised strategy, and mental strength, one can overcome all ebbs and flows. Just like the ocean can be daunting, so can the market; and just like surfers can adapt to altering weather conditions, we traders can adapt to changing market conditions.

Allow me to draw attention to the difference between being resilient and being stubborn as hell, a mistake that traders and surfers both make. I'm sure by now, most of us have heard Einstein's famous line, "Insanity is doing the same thing over and over again and expecting different results." If you find yourself nearing this point, please take a break, go back to basics, switch to learning mode, research what you need to do differently, or maybe seek professional guidance.

Honesty is another essential ingredient for a good surfer; which is also true for traders too. Some use their flaws or limitations as an excuse to procrastinate; instead, view them as a mirror of your potential and endless possibilities. Austrian neurologist and founder of psychoanalysis, Sigmund Freud once said, "Being entirely honest with oneself is a good exercise." If you can't be honest with yourself, recognize your strengths and identify your weaknesses, how will you ever grow? Assess yourself regularly, be vulnerable, be transparent, and seek professional guidance if needed.

Good surfers are always respectful and thankful for opportunities granted to them by the ocean. Similarly, good traders should always be respectful and thankful for what the market provides us. Greed is not your friend; we need to learn to appreciate every ounce of progress and celebrate every little milestone. This is the secret to long-term growth, success, and fulfillment in life.

Mental performance addresses the psychology of sports performance, which is why most pro athletes have coaches to help them increase confidence, handle the high demands of training, perform well under pressure, and overcome adversity. Most of us have either seen or heard of pro athletes who suddenly choke before a competition. Yes, diamonds are made under pressure—but so are mental breakdowns. The more sustainable way is to let success be the consequence of your practice, instead of the end goal itself. This applies to traders as well, especially ones who lose sight of their disciplined practice—sidetracked by their daydreams of success. Don't confuse this slippery slope, full of frustrations and the search for instant gratification—with ambition, my friend. We should be ambitious, while setting realistic, meaningful, attainable, measurable short- and long- term goals. What do beginner wave-surfers and stock market surfers need to know?

Safety Guide: The ocean can be a dangerous place for surfers, just like the market can be for traders. Fortunately, there are methodical ways to navigate rough waters. Like surfers, traders can educate themselves on how to stay safe and avoid dangerous situations.

Essential Swimming Skills: A prerequisite of surfing is to first be a proficient swimmer. With trading, you can also learn how to walk before you run; develop a disciplined trading system and stick to it, use charts to identify trading signals/price patterns, understand basic market psychology, and identify profitable opportunities. I had to get it all wrong before learning (the hard way) how to do it right; impulse-control and more mechanical/less emotional entering/managing of trading positions are indispensable skills.

Rip Currents: These strong narrow channels of water rush from the beach back to the ocean. Some rip currents can be extremely powerful and are always present, even if you don't see them. This is why surfers need to understand how to identify and adapt to them. Surfers can either ride out the rip current, save their energy and swim/surf back to shore—OR they can panic, try to swim against the current, exhaust themselves, and possibly drown. Sound familiar? Traders need to know how to identify gap ups, gap downs, dips and crashes when they begin to emerge. They also need to know how to react if caught in one—because they can either respond in a calm and collected way—OR they can freak out, abandon their strategy and possibly go bankrupt.

Surf Conditions: All surfers must be able to differentiate between beach breaks (where the waves break over a sandy bottom), point breaks (where the wave hits a piece of land that sticks out and gradually rolls toward shore) and reef breaks (where beautiful, sharp coral reefs form under shallow water). Beach breaks with lifeguards are recommended for beginners, while reef breaks are recommended for intermediate or advanced surfers. Similarly, beginner traders should start small, focusing on a maximum of one or two stocks at a time.

I had a bit of beginner's luck starting off only trading Amazon stocks. I can't say that it was a conscious decision, but I do remember Amazon stock just felt more beginner-friendly, like soft and sandy beach breaks. They exhibited low volatility, gentle waters, and a general sense of comfort—being one of the top 10 largest companies with stock held by many big investors. On the other hand, penny stocks, that most retail traders bet on, resembles a reef break; high risk of coral cuts and serious infections. Beginner surfers may find its "barrels" (hollow waves) alluring, however, they're also called "plunging waves" because they can pick people up and dump them onto a shallow area. Novice swimmers and traders alike, risk losing their lives if not careful.

So, I humbly appeal that you always keep your guard up and stay on your toes!

Timing: The surf forecast can change significantly, hour by hour and day by day. On top of that, no two waves are identical. As a beginner, one day could be extremely discouraging, while the next day could be highly pleasing. Every surfer needs to learn how to read waves, predict how they will break, and decide if they will (A) follow the wave to their right, (B) follow the wave to their left, (C) catch a closeout within 1-2 seconds, (D) go straight, (E) turn around and paddle or (F) wipeout—hard. Similarly, market conditions are constantly changing; many factors can influence market trends, which is why a solid trading system (trade preparation, technical analysis, entry rules, exit rules, and time frame) is so incredibly crucial.

Like beginner surfers, beginner traders will have good days and bad days. On our bad days, we have a choice; we can either (A) allow anxiety and self-defeating thoughts to destroy us or (B) shake it off, learn this lesson for your next opportunity, and wake up wiser the next day. Easier said than done, I know, which is why we need to establish SOPs (standard operating procedures) first. This way, when things like this happen, we can look at our battle plan and remember what to do next. That sounds way better than activating the negativity effect, when one block falls, and all the others follow—like a domino effect). I've placed a treasure trove at the end of this chapter. Don't miss it, my friend.

Choosing the Right Surfboard: Surfers should choose their boards after accurately calculating their ideal surfboard size/volume (as there are variables such as height, weight, age, and surfing level). Matching one's abilities to the right board makes it easier for surfers of all levels to learn, surf, balance, control, paddle, and catch waves. Similarly, every trader needs a good trading platform; one that provides insights, education, and tools to help you navigate the market and learn essential techniques. I was fortunate enough to be trained on thinkorswim®. While I also like a few other platforms (for their simplicity, etc.), thinkorswim® is the best one, in my opinion.

Land Training: Beginner surfers are recommended to start with land-based training. This allows them to get a feel of the movements and build muscle memory, without introducing bad habits, before literally getting their feet wet—out on the water. Similarly, my mistake of skipping properly practicing with paper trading first was super off the mark. This was definitely one of the causes of my slow start and stunted progress. Never underestimate the power of practice theory.

Protective Gear: It's public knowledge that there are many surfers who chase adrenaline and take unnecessary risks. However, real pros, especially the ones who have ended up in hospital beds, know the importance of safety equipment. For example: surf helmets (to prevent brain injury), reef boots (protection from rocks and coral), wetsuits (to prevent hypothermia), board leashes (helps you surface after a wipeout), and ear plugs (to prevent exostosis—abnormal bone growths that constrict the ear canal). Similarly, us traders need to protect ourselves! One key rule of mine was, "Never risk more than 1-2% of my principal when entering a trade." Follow my guidelines in previous chapters around all the aspects of how I protect myself from losing my shirt.

Observe and Learn: Surfers keep improving and learning, using a valuable skill—observing themselves and others. Similarly, traders need to keep learning and improving, observing the outcomes of each of their trades. Avoid abandoning your functioning strategy just because you're losing focus or "bored.". Stick with what works and revise as you find the need. There's no harm in going back to the basics if you suddenly discover that you've strayed from the plan without realizing.

Patience: Surfers know that if they miss a wave, there will always be another one soon. The ocean makes more than enough waves all day, every day, for every surfer to catch a wave. They understand that there's no need to be concerned whether another wave will come or not; they just need to wait patiently for the next one. Regrettably watching the missed wave go causes them to miss the next one. Similarly, the market regularly generates trends; if you miss one, just patiently wait for the next one. I hope that you will not waste your time or energy on regret, my friend.

Have Fun: The simplest and most underrated one of all—great advice that applies to everything we do. Finding ways to make your work fun (without losing focus) not only helps you stay energized, reduce stress levels, and avoid burnout but also has a positive impact on your creativity and purpose! Think about it, instead of dreading your to-do list, what if you're eager to dig in and complete them? Be creative; this can mean anything from decorating your workspace with things that bring you joy (like plants or wall art), rewarding yourself (with an affordable monitor or comfy office chair), to networking with like-minded industry professionals! When we allow joy and work to coexist, we become resilient.

Rinse and Repeat: Surfing a few times each season won't foster progress, it requires commitment, if you wish to advance. The more you practice, the easier it becomes and the better you get. The better you get, the more fun you have. The more fun you have, the more you want to go surfing! Read that again, my friend. This is exactly the same for traders; trading requires commitment and routine practice.

Recover After Wipeouts: No matter how experienced a surfer is, they may still wipeout, need to bail, or get locked in a heavy wave, due to unexpected encounters from time to time. Even if they make every effort to ride the wave and kick-out, they may still end up in a washing machine (getting tossed around underwater). Both life and trading are full of "washing machine" moments; it hurts, you're scared and you don't know if you will get out of this. This is when your "bounce-back" skills will come in really handy. Remember "the battle plan"? If you were paying attention and took my words to heart, then, when you were developing your trading strategies, you would have also developed strategies to deal with loss. They will serve as your map, with directions to the light at the end of every tunnel.

Acceptance: When surfers screw up, they accept responsibility and don't waste time or energy spiraling. Usually, they will collect themselves, go home, rest for a day or week. Then, they will realign their focus and rebuild their confidence through practice, perhaps at a different beach with calmer water. The same goes for traders, if the market kicks your butt, take a break. Just like a surfer wouldn't stay and fight the ocean, you don't need to stay and fight the market. A break will allow you to recuperate, accept that no one wins 100% of the time, and come back stronger and wiser. Have you ever heard of the saying, "You can't pour from an empty cup"? This is why self-care is of vital importance.

Regardless of whether you're a beginner or returning trader, just like those learning a new language: (1) Knowledge retention requires repeat exposure of new information, (2) repetition and retrieval practice, and (3) accept that there's no shortcut to creating neural pathways in your brain, also known as "Ctrl+S".

My net profit was only around $12,000 at the time. How did I reach a six-figure profit and not only lose it all but also incur a net loss in six-figures? Don't miss out on the Easter eggs hidden in the remaining chapters.

POP QUIZ:

Q: What is self-care?
A: Here's my treasure trove of "Rainy Day Reminders." Please repeat after me:

(1) This is temporary, things will get better, it won't be like this forever. (I promise)

(2) I will remind myself: "One day, I can tell the story of the mountain I climbed; my words could become a page in someone else's survival guide." (Inspired by Morgan Harper Nichols)

(3) If I don't pick time for self-care, my body will pick it for me. Self-care is good for both my body and mind. This could mean: a 30 or 60-minute brisk nature walk, get some fresh air and feel the sun on my face, take a long hot shower, meditate, get enough sleep, cook/eat a nutritious meal, dance in the kitchen, or make time for healthy activities that bring me joy—like going on a hike/swim with a friend. (Or all of the above)

(4) I will talk to myself like I would to someone I love (inspired by Brené Brown). I will not allow a bully to live in my head. I will practice positive self-talk so my negativity doesn't lead to a self-fulfilling prophecy. I will encourage, motivate, and be nice to myself.

SPECIAL MENTION: SHORT & CONCISE CHAPTER SERIES

"Not that the story need be long, but it will take a long while to make it short."

—Henry David Thoreau

The next several chapters are going to be noticeably short and concise. I was debating perhaps combining them into one chapter and creating topics within the chapter; however, after much thought, I decided that each of these topics have gained enough respect to stand on its own. While my stories may be concise, there's still room for yours; because if you don't learn from my mistakes, you'll be back to write your stories next to mine. However, if you manage to absorb these principles, we'll be able to keep your stories off my book!

I have intentionally left a blank space here so you can come back and write your success or lessons learned next to mine. Isn't that a great idea?

Take the opportunity to read and master the concepts and learnings from this book. don't let the market fool you. I'm sure you've heard the saying, "Fool me once, shame on you; Fool me twice, shame on me!"

CHAPTER 5
FOCUS ON WHAT YOU CAN CONTROL: THE DESERTER

"Trying to trade during a losing streak is emotionally devastating. Trying to play 'catch-up' is lethal."

—Ed Seykota

There are things you can control and then there are things that you cannot. I effectively rode the market trends on Amazon stock during the first months of 2018 and generated almost $12,000 in profits. So, why did I miss my goal of $25,000 for 2018? Around the middle of 2018, my mother had another severe health incident. I had to take a few weeks off from my consulting day job to focus on the home front. My emotional state was not at its best, so I decided to stay away from trading, but I'd still spend some time to make sure I didn't completely get out of touch with my skills. Several weeks passed and I didn't make a single trade. It became obvious that a sick family member was my Kryptonite, my mental health really took a nosedive.

A few weeks later, my mother recovered to a decent level and I immediately resumed my consulting job. My manager was kind enough to support my home situation. I had some catch-up to do at work while still giving time to my family, this caused a further delay in my resuming trading. I used my time during weekends and evenings to learn more about the state of the market instead of trading. I wanted to learn more, so I reached out to Guru, and he helped me with several new, intriguing strategies and things he had learned about the market. This kept me engaged to a level; however, I didn't realize that I was slowly losing touch with the discipline that I'd started to build in trading (during the early part of 2018).

Gradually, I caught up. I also started to earn decent money from my consulting gig and put aside some savings. I decided to increase the size of my trades, which would also mean an additional risk of losses. In hindsight, it also exposed me to the rewards of profit. If I remember correctly, from twenty-five Amazon stocks, I went on to trade a maximum of fifty-five Amazon stocks. I know fifty-five is an odd number, I could have done 50, but that was probably the maximum I could go with the trading balance that I built up, along with some day trading margins. I was trying out margins for the first time.

A word of extreme caution: You should only tap into margins if you've been an extremely disciplined trader with years of successful trading. At first, tapping into margins feels like grabbing new money, but it's a trap. The thought of needing to catch up on several months of lost trading time consumed me, because lost opportunities meant lost dollars. So, I decided to switch things up with my strategy and added a couple of new charts. These charts were added to help further my understanding of market trends and spot trade triggers. *According to Trades That Swing, "A trade trigger is a precise event that tells you to get into or out of a trade, right now. It helps avoid getting in or out too early, too late, skipping trades, or taking trades you shouldn't."* This became the new setup, after becoming more comfortable by watching the charts, I decided it was time to resume trading.

I continued to mostly trade Amazon, while keeping an eye on a few other stocks I'd recently added to my charts. I should've been more confident with my trades with my new setup. However, I noticed myself hesitating when taking a trade, my mind had to process a few more steps than I was used to. After a few test trades, going back to my original simple setup felt like the right thing to do, so I did. The reason I'd strayed from my original setup was because it felt like the market wasn't providing enough opportunities (meaning: I lost my patience). The cycle of watching the market, looking for a setup, and then psyching myself out continued. You see, impatience and greed got to my head. I allowed the temptation of the new setup with potentially valuable indicators to distract me.

The right thing to do would have been to either stay the course, stick with my original setup and give it a chance—OR commit time towards practicing the new setup via a trading simulator. PSA: It's okay to build a new setup if it improves predictability. It's ok to try out a new setup if you've matured as a trader and feel ready for the next step. What's NOT okay is to dive into a new setup without adequate practice. Isn't this true for all new ventures we want to undertake?

Finally, I decided to abandon my original trading setup and jump ship to the new one—to pursue the value that I desperately craved. My mind continued to struggle with processing information. Now, instead of two or three steps, my brain had to process five or six procedures before making a trade. After spending some time training myself, I found I was comfortable handling three or four steps, and from there, I was able to gradually take on one or two additional tasks for optimum effectiveness. The details of this modified setup is irrelevant, because I moved away from it after a couple of years. My winning streak broke and by the end of 2018, I'd missed my goal of earning $25,000 from trading that year.

In today's episode of "Please, Learn from my Mistakes, I Beg You!":

- Don't abandon a functional ship (or trading system) that was built with your blood, sweat, and tears.
- There's beauty in keeping things simple if it works. After all, Leonardo Di Vinci once said, "Simplicity is the ultimate sophistication."
- Everyone is different; what works for others may not work for you—and vice versa.

- Discovering what works best for you requires you to have new eyes and rewire your brain.
- Patience is a virtue, my friend, good things are worth waiting for.
- Missing out is part of the game; embrace it, or you'll miss even more.
- Keep your focus on your functioning trading system, not money; it's easier said than done, but it will benefit you in the long run.
- Stay focused; ensure the system and strategies you created is working like a well-oiled machine.
- Continue to execute and repeat your SOP (Standard Operating Procedure) until you reach automation. According to Rutgers, "Automated behaviors increase the likelihood of success because many people are simply too busy, too undisciplined, or both (to oversee their diet and finances on a daily basis)."
- Electric robots can run out of power too, don't forget to recharge yourself to avoid burnout.
- Hope for the best and prepare for the worst.
- Emotional regulation skills will save your life: According to Very Well Mind, "Healthy emotion regulation includes components such as: (1) The ability to recognize that you're having an emotional response and to understand what that response is. (2) Accepting your emotional responses rather than rejecting them or reacting to them with fear. This can be difficult even for people who don't have BPD, as emotions such as anger or sadness are often discouraged by society. (3) The ability to access strategies that allow you to reduce the intensity of the emotion you're feeling when you need to. This means if someone has

enraged you, you don't give in to the desire to physically lash out at them or hurl a long line of epithets their way. In fact, when you're upset, you should be able to engage in goal-directed behavior if you're well-versed in emotion regulation. (4) The ability to control impulsive behaviors when you're upset. If you feel like trashing your home because you received upsetting news, you can curb the inclination to throw everything on the floor or punch a hole in the wall.

POP QUIZ:

Q: What is a trade trigger?
A: Signs to watch for that indicate when to promptly get into or out of a trade.

CHAPTER 6
LACK OF COMMITMENT: THE SPECTATOR

"There is a difference between interest and commitment. When you are interested in doing something, you do it only when it is convenient. When you are committed to something, you accept no excuses, only results."

—Kenneth Blanchard

In the end of 2018, for several reasons, I transitioned from a contract employment to a full-time position at my day job. My workload increased significantly, which required me to do overtime. It felt rewarding, so I didn't mind it. However, I made an effort to be mindful of my health, as I knew that if it was neglected, it would directly impact my ability to work, get paid, and support my mother and sister.

Between work and home, it was extremely challenging for me to fit anything else into the mix in 2019. Since I was swamped, I started to wonder if it was wise to continue trading. What if I suddenly can't keep my head above water and my work or family suffers? At that time, I didn't realize there was another factor warding me off continuing to trade. Now, looking back, I see that my 2018 profits were not motivating enough for me to justify spending so much time on it in this new year.

The truth is, trading was becoming more of an interest than a discipline, my commitment had waned. Gradually, I switched from a devoted moonlighting day trader to a swing trader. Swing traders trade less frequently and hold positions for days or weeks. My strategy changed to swing trading time frames. I began to observe the market and try to predict where the market was headed in the next five to twenty days; buying and holding stock positions based on my observations and predictions, then selling them whenever I saw them approaching a certain level. This is a risky method if swing trading with penny or highly volatile stocks; I'd advise against it, which is why my swing trading consisted of some of the most stable stocks. Note: the stocks in the bull market would never dip noticeably on consecutive days, they usually went up slowly but surely. There's a strategy for trading these types of stocks, which I'll touch on briefly near the end of this book.

There were days when even my so-called low-risk stocks dipped and didn't perform as forecasted via my trading system. The key issue with my swing trading system was that I never established a stop loss, this is a dangerous game to play in day trading, friends. As day traders, we should always, ALWAYS pre-determine a stop loss and apply it when conditions require us to do so. Traders who miss this golden rule will likely drain their accounts someday (in the near future).

A few of my swing trades tanked as a result of sudden market volatility and I incurred apparent losses, it broke my 2% profit level and 1% loss level exit strategy. Once, I even swung into an almost 10% loss, after missing a couple days of watching the market for my swing trades. This setback raised alarm bells, alerting me to pause and re-evaluate my approach, leading me to spend much more time observing the market off-hours and on weekends. Soon after, I reached out to Guru and asked him what he was up to. He was kind enough to share many new learnings regarding the stock market, the options market, futures, and even some aspects of forex. It was evident then, that I should use every opportunity to learn from Guru as much as possible.

Trading no longer felt like my passion, my fear of sustaining any more losses was crippling me. Too many factors were impacting my ability to analyze data objectively, including the health of my mother, sister, and myself. I told myself that the timing wasn't right, I didn't have enough time during the week, I only had one or two hours on weekends, so I should just let up and go into learning mode for now. It's obvious to me now that these were all excuses that could've been overcome with discipline and improved mental health. What I needed to do was identify the fear of sustaining another loss and the fact that I'd been fed with false hope. The truth is, my losses occurred because I strayed from my trading system, by not setting up a stop loss, it's as simple as that.

Not to mention, I was also lured into crypto exchanges. The reason why I started to branch out into crypto was because its market was always open and more active on weekends, which worked better for me as I had my plate full on weekdays. Although crypto isn't the topic of this book, it's worth a mention because some weekend crypto exchanges using my basic trading system worked well and earned me around $200 every weekend. However, eventually, my brain clicked into long-term investment mode and I held onto all my crypto, becoming more of a spectator than a crypto or stock trader, and that was the end of my crypto journey for 2019!

Ultimately, 2019 turned out to be a washout year for me as far as trading went. I probably needed this break to see things through a different lens, after getting a taste of watching millions changing hands in the market. My covert greed for making quick money was sprouting within me; an unfamiliar trait that I never knew existed was slowly beginning to hijack me.

POP QUIZ:

Q: Upon entering a position, a good trader should ALWAYS pre-determine a _________ and apply it when necessary.
A: STOP-LOSS!

CHAPTER 7
MOONLIGHTING TRADER: THE RESURGENT

"A peak performance trader is totally committed to being the best and doing whatever it takes to be the best. He feels totally responsible for whatever happens and thus can learn from mistakes. These people typically have a working business plan for trading because they treat trading as a business."

—Van K. Tharp

2019 was a great teacher; the much-needed break gave me time to reassess everything. I had a realization; I needed to release the pressure that I'd placed on myself—to make money from each trade. I had to remind myself, again, that the goal as a trader is to make the best trades, not to earn the highest return possible. Also, I needed to remember not to lose more than 1% of my principal in one trade.

Another revelation occurred: I should've never started trading without a day job. Four to six months of savings didn't get me enough time to learn the A-Zs of trading—while naively unaware of the significance of trading discipline. During those four to six months, I desperately pushed myself to make it work. This resulted in one derailment after another, as I continued to search for shortcuts and make impulsive, emotional decisions.

It was becoming clear to me that the right way to start trading as a beginner—is to do it as a side gig, in tandem with a stable full-time job. Once you've acquired skills, discipline, and a positive experience via your trading demo account—then you must evaluate your progress. None of these steps may be missed before going into day trading 100%. Demo accounts allow you to buy and sell virtual stocks (using paper trading) and test them under real-time market conditions; without losing your shirt. This is the perfect practice for beginners as they continue to work their day jobs.

You may be surprised to find that there are tons of profitable opportunities via after hours trading. You can successfully plan your trades days in advance and simply set automated alerts or even automated purchase points for low-risk trades (with stop loss points set). Just avoid trading on days when market conditions are extremely volatile, if you're unable to watch the market in real-time. Alternatively, you can trade futures (24/7), which are traded in contracts and not shares like stocks. However, this isn't something one should get into without knowledge of (1) how futures markets work, (2) speculating and leveraging positions, (3) hedging against losses, and of course, (4) emotional control of fear, anxiety, and greed.

So, what did I end up doing after 2019? Well, I view 2020 as a year that will never be forgotten, for many reasons. 2020 completely changed the world on so many levels. As soon as the lockdowns started, the world as we knew it ground to a halt—and so did the markets. The market entered a new era of volatility and unpredictability for all long-, mid-, and short-term investors. It seemed dollar-cost averaging was the only strategy left, for investors to reduce the impact of volatility by spreading out purchases over time, instead of buying shares at a high point. This mutated environment was challenging even for day traders, but doable for the ones who followed a proven system.

The pandemic resulted in remote work. This helped me, as I was saving almost two to three hours of commute time daily. Additionally, the workload that was demanding extra hours started to taper down in 2020. The first half of that year was a bit chaotic. I must confess, I was fearful of the pandemic; concerned for the health of my immunocompromised family members. The first half of 2020 was, again, a wash—in terms of trading. Due to my emotional state, caused by the pandemic and the focus on my family, I missed a major market opportunity.

A couple of months into the pandemic, I was finally able to pull myself together and decided to shift my focus towards becoming a moonlighting trader. This was the first, long-overdue emergence of a trading system; one that would gradually mature and benefit any trader who sticks to its discipline. Nobody's ever won a war without a battle plan, my friend. Looking back on all the hurdles, barriers, stumbling blocks, obstacles, drawbacks, deterrents—you get the point (ha-ha)—that I'd faced, it was time to finally figure out the best course of action for me. I bounced some ideas off of Guru and he had some valuable insights for me. Sometimes, it all starts with only a pen and paper; this is what I put together:

What will I trade?

- Stocks
- Futures
- Options

When will I trade?

- Pre-market: Stocks (Amazon, Apple, or TQQQ).
- Post-market: Stocks (Amazon, Apple, or TQQQ).
- Overnight: Futures (Micro E-minis S&P 500 futures).
- Weekend Prep: Options (Amazon, Apple, or TQQQ).
- Market Hours (on personal days off): Options with "0-5 DTE" (under 5 days to expiration).

How long will I hold my trades?

- Swing Trading Stocks (2-5 days max).
- Same-day Trading Stocks (15–30 min max).
- Swing Trading Options (4-6 weeks).
- Same-week Trading Options (0-5 DTE).
- Futures (evenings and nights).

How frequently will I trade?

- Time permitting (daily or weekly but at minimum 2 days per week)
- Trade setup must always be present, in order to proceed with a trade.

How will I stay focused?

- Rehearse my trading system daily, for at least 15-20 minutes.
- Even if I don't make a trade that day, I can still mentally practice the steps.
- Follow my trading system religiously; STICK TO THE RULES!!!

What will I do with my profits on a bi-weekly basis?

- Invest 5% of my profits into mid-term (1-2 years expiry) options.
- Invest 40% of my profits into both long-term dividend stocks and ETFs.
- Donate 5% of my profits to a cause close to my heart.
- Cash out 30% into the bank.
- Hold 20% in my account = risk management.
- Re-invest dividend earnings into buying fractional stablecoins or emerging market stocks.

What will my new and improved "trade setup" be?

- Build on previous rules (listed in Chapter 3; please revisit to refresh your memory).
- When a short period EMA crosses above the long period EMA, take a BUY position, and when a short period EMA crosses below the long period EMA, take a SELL position. The ideal values of short and long periods are 5 and 20, respectively.
- Set up one chart in 5-minute intervals and one in 15-minute intervals (side-by-side).

- Trading volume is not a concern because of my stock selection, but still good to watch, especially since a huge spike can be a super-trend indicator.
- Number of stocks per trade will be 50 or 100, depending on the price.
- No changes to my support and resistance strategy for profit taking or cutting losses.
- Add one more layer of reassurance for decision-making in volatile conditions, using the RSI (Relative Strength Index) Indicator. This will help me identify securities that are (1) overbought or oversold, (2) about to have a trend reversal, or (3) corrective price pullback. *Consider overbought when RSI above 80 and oversold when below 20*
- Only trade on days that display a comfortable setup.

So, how did I do in 2020? Well, I made over $25K in profits following this day trading discipline (during the remaining 5-6 months of 2020). Although, not long after this, I realized that I'd developed a very greedy way of choosing investment stocks and crypto.

POP QUIZ:

Q: Why didn't I elaborate on any other technical strategies and indicators for trade setup?
A: There are many technical indicators and strategies out there for your trading toolkit. If you want to learn more, YouTube is your friend. Some examples are mentioned in later chapters; occasionally I'll also post on Rewired.Guru. I urge you to find a strategy that suits you, that you can stick to.

CHAPTER 8
WALL STREET "DISTRICT" BETS: THE BETTORS

"I think I am safe in asserting that the margin trader, speculator, gambler, or whatever you choose to designate the average man who goes to Wall Street after easy money, does not lose money when he sells. He loses it when he buys!"

—Edwin Lefevre

In 2020, I fared decently overall, and was starting to feel more confident with trading. I must confess, I was disciplined, but not entirely consistent. My goal was to reach a level where my trading discipline would become my second nature, I quickly realized that it was not going to be easy. We humans are complex, emotional beings, our minds need to be reined in from all the shiny distractions. This is how you keep your eye on the ball and hit a home run.

I used to always try and stay on top of real-time financial market coverage, without getting overly influenced by the news. I'd rather buckle down and focus on my trading system strategies, regardless of what the stock market news would report. *According to Investopedia, "A trading strategy is the method of buying and selling in markets that is based on predefined rules used to make trading decisions."* Right around this time, a retail traders' group online made it onto the news. This group caught my attention; it had achieved major strides and made a killing day trading options and stocks.

Greed emerged and began to take control of me, it was bent on making some quick money. Hence, I was captivated by the news of this retail online trading group and promptly joined the group on social media. A notification informed me that I was declined from the group, I guess there's a first time for everything.

Apparently, they had become a closed group for the time-being. I was so disappointed, I really wanted to be a part of that group; the reports of their accomplishments, enticed my urge to make some quick money. After a few weeks, I learned that they opened the group up again. I gladly joined the group and started to follow the action, on and off, whenever I had time to do so. Until the end of 2020, this group was more of a source of curiosity and entertainment for me than anything else.

In early 2021, for the first three months, I continued to stick to my trading discipline. I probably made another $12K in those 3 months and felt happy about my progress. The beginning of April brought some unexpected tough times. Unfortunately, one late night, my mother had the worst fall of her life. Prior to this, her health had already been deteriorating day by day. Her fall that night and the scream I heard, still shakes me, even to this day. My mother was immediately rushed to the hospital and I stayed there with her for almost 10 days. This occurred during the start of another wave of the pandemic. It was incredibly challenging, I had no choice but to be with her, in the hospital, for the majority of that time. Not only did I have to take a family emergency leave of absence from my day job, but I also struggled to witness the pillar of strength in my life, fighting for her own life.

Everyone knows that our time here has an expiration date, but that didn't make it any easier for me to watch my mother suffer, I felt so unbelievably helpless. Due to being on my feet so much, while caring for my mother, I ended up developing an unexpected infection in my legs, which caused me to also require immediate medical attention. After that, I continued to be at the hospital, tending to my mother, until her doctors delivered the news that it was time for her to transition to hospice care. They told me to bring her home, where home care would provide hospice care. This was the hardest time of my life.

Following the move, she spent the last couple days of her life at home, she was at peace. To be honest, I had been preparing myself for her passing, for a few years already, and took every additional day I got with her as a gift. However, when I actually lost her, I could not cope, it almost broke me. She was my cornerstone, my anchor, my safe harbor, all of those things and more. While I was thankful that I was able to spend so much time with her during the last few years, I still felt like I could have done so much more for her.

Too many things happened all at once, my sister could not cope with the loss of our mother, and her health significantly deteriorated too. This series of events compounded and the emotional toll began to feel unbearable. I tried my best to stay in control but it wasn't long before my doctor put me on steroids and anxiety medication. I suffered multiple panic attacks over the course of several months and had to take an extended leave of absence from my day job, due to my poor mental health. I felt lost, unsure of my purpose in life, and started seeking my "ikigai." *According to positivepsychology.com, Ikigai (ee-key-guy) is a Japanese concept that combines the terms "iki", meaning "alive" or "life," and gai, meaning "benefit" or "worth."*

It took me a couple of months to get my bearings. Around June of 2021, I returned to my day job, after my doctor gave me the green light. After a gap of almost 3 months, I finally started to look at the stock market again. I believe this was sometime in July, when I started to refresh my memory about how to resume trading. I was extremely desperate at the time, to increase my income and make a difference in my sister's life. Her health was declining and I was not ready to watch her suffer like my mother did. I needed to help her improve her quality of life, so she could live a normal life, despite the limitations put on her, due to her health condition.

During this time, I did not realize that I was nowhere close to being emotionally ready to resume trading; I was still struggling with anxiety. On top of that, I was functioning under tremendous pressure to make some quick, big money. At that time, I decided to quit trading, because I was convinced that it wasn't going to rake in the big bucks soon enough. At this point, my "low-risk" mindset switched to "high-risk" mode. I convinced myself," High risk means high reward!" This was not the disciplined me anymore. This is when I remembered the online retail trading group that I joined in 2020 and decided to log back in to check out what was going on. I was an introvert the entire time, not actively participating in the group, only reading and listening to what was happening, through this group. To my surprise, being a part of this group helped me by providing the distraction I needed from all the stress I had just gone through.

While observing this group, I noticed a collection of members, who were actively trading on earnings. They called it "Earnings Play," a day trading strategy for stocks and options. For some reason, this caught my attention. Why? Because there were opportunities of huge 10x multipliers with options. At the same time, it had equal risks of losing big. Without really thinking about it, I decided to give earnings plays a try. I selected a couple of upcoming earnings stocks—and as luck would have it, I made over $12K in profit overnight from my first earnings play. I know, you're probably thinking, "Wait, did I read that right? Did he just say that he made over $12K in profit, overnight?" Yes, that's what I said! That amount would take three months to earn with my trading discipline of "low risk-low rewards."

That win was a major boost for me, I was thrilled. I felt like the $12K was going to grow even more, so I decided to keep holding the position and didn't exit—taking the profits. Remember when I told you that it's important to know when to take profits and when to cut losses? Well, I completely threw all of that advice out the door. That earnings play kept going up and I was over $16K in profit, so I kept holding the position. The next day, something happened, the stock price dropped, and I was only left with $8K in profit. I decided to keep holding it, and hoped it was just a pullback, and I'd win big with this one. Well, it never turned back, and I lost all the profits that I was sitting on because I didn't stick to my trading discipline.

"So, did you learn your lesson, Shiv?" You ask. No, I was not ready to admit my negligence. I kept repeating the same mistake, over and over again; making random entries into stocks and options, based on the opinions in this retail trading group. After a while, I finally realized that I was heavily influenced by this group, it was becoming my evening and weekend addiction. How did this happen? Well, I believe all the funny posts were serving as a distraction for me. Moreover, being a part of this group gave me hope of hitting the jackpot one of those days. What I didn't realize was that the group predominantly consisted of smart bettors! That is why earnings play is one of their strengths, other than something called meme stocks (basically stocks that have gone viral).

It was fascinating to see millions of new members swarm into this group each month, like bees to honey. Let me tell you, at one point, this group had a mix of people with all the different phases that I had gone through. There were gamblers, bettors, braggers, grabbers, borrowers, debtors, slackers, HODLers, defamers, losers, hopefuls, copycats, listeners, learners, surfers, sailors, and lastly, non-starters. It was a melting pot of trading identities. You name it, they had it.

I must have gone through a dozen of those phases over the course of a few months, before I came to my senses. Why didn't I just stick to my trading discipline? Alternatively, I could have used the power of this group to strengthen my trading system, instead of ignorantly throwing everything I knew out the window. Today, I'm thankful to be a part of this group. Ultimately, it led to the flourishing of my expertise. Not to mention, due to my lack of discipline when I first joined this group, I got carried away and sustained a great loss. My lapse in judgment had me senselessly chasing everything on the market. These types of Wall Street retail traders' groups are like a double-edged sword. If you're someone who's super disciplined, focused, and unemotional, you may benefit from this group via staying informed about trending opportunities.

Back when I used to go to the bar with my buddies, I was always the designated driver. To my female friends, I was the best shopping companion, as I was a great window shopper. I also loved going to casinos, but never played more than $20 per visit. If you are someone who can go to the bar, resist drinking and drive responsibly; avoid retail therapy; go to a casino and resist gambling; then it's probably safe for you to join the group. I hope you get the gist; success in day trading isn't achievable without being disciplined. However, if you're able to resist temptations of this sort (the group), there's a good chance you'll be able to advance in leaps and bounds. You just need to be disciplined to only bet with what you can afford to lose. Watch for the right signal in this group, get on the market trend train, and exit before that train reverses its course.

In the next few chapters, I'm going to touch on my slip-ups, while alternating between various identities as a trader, hooked to this group without a purpose. Please don't be like me and make these extremely costly mistakes. Granted, I have emerged from the repercussions, but why endure that kind of agony, if you can learn from my mistakes?

RECAP:

- Profits from trading since joining this group: 6-figures
- Losses from trading since joining this group: 6-figures, twice.
- Net profit from trading since joining this group: 6-figure loss.
- Lessons learned: Well, this book speaks to it all!

POP QUIZ:

Q: Who is to blame?

A: Not the group; me. I didn't stick to my discipline, period. That shiny pot of gold at the end of the rainbow turned out to be my weakness, in the midst of my desperation to financially aid my sister.

CHAPTER 9
FOOL'S GOLD: THE DAREDEVIL

"In trading, you must be defensive and aggressive at the same time. If you are not aggressive, you are not going to make money and if you are not defensive, you are not going to keep money."

—Ray Dalio

Every opportunity I had was used to keep learning more about the stock market, this was when I came across TQQQ, one of the largest leveraged ETFs (exchange traded funds) that also tracks the Nasdaq-100 (a capitalization-weighted index that tracks more than 3700 stocks, owned by 100 of the largest companies on Nasdaq—the world's first electronic exchange—listing most of the world's tech giants). TQQQ is suitable for day traders because of their short-holding periods. Learning that triple leverage could provide triple returns in bull markets placed dollar signs in my eyes. On the other hand, this also means losses will be tripled, so watch out!

This ETF was ideal for me because even on a dull market day, trading TQQQ gave me more edge in my strategy. For long-term buy-and-hold investors, QQQ is a good choice; broad, low cost, liquid and actively traded. For those who are not familiar with leveraged ETF, like the TQQQ, which is "triple-leveraged", meaning it returns 3 times the index. For example: if the Nasdaq-100 rises 1%, then the TQQQ will increase 3%. Similarly, if the Nasdaq-100 falls 1%, then the TQQQ will decrease by 3%. So, it's fair to say that my decision to trade TQQQ was a little aggressive. However, the tangible trading action that was available to me any time of the day, including pre- and post- market, was super helpful (for me).

The triple leverage began to shine quick money potential. Over time, I started to explore more and more available leveraged

ETFs that were triple or double. Gradually, I compiled a list of those that appealed to me and here are some that I added to my portfolio: FNGU, BULZ, NUGT, GDXU, AGQ, TQQQ, SOXL, and LABU. Yup, you heard right, I was building my portfolio with triple leveraged ETFs because I couldn't resist that shimmering triple return—and fooled myself. You know, in the case of a bear market, holding them in your portfolio as investments could empty your account 3x the speed. Risk long-term investment in these leveraged stocks very wisely, by timing them for short or mid-term investments.

Choosing these leveraged long-term investments in an attempt to make some quick money, instead of logically using them for day trading or short-term swing trading, really kicked my butt. You should be very well versed in leveraged ETFs before investing in them long-term, I'd highly caution you against tapping into these. Trust me, I learned the hard way; after losing over 50% of the principal invested into each leveraged ETF, just holding them in volatile/bear markets. No stop loss involved either; I assumed that was the way to approach long-term investments, without realizing that what one should do is utilize a more solid strategy (when selecting stocks, index funds or ETFs).

Not only is leveraging a dicey strategy for long-term investments it's also pretty touch-and-go in day trading or swing trading, if you don't follow the strict discipline of minimizing your losses. A stop loss strategy is especially critical for leveraged trades, the same goes for penny or parabolic stocks, my friends. We'll discuss those ones in a later chapter.

My rationale behind creating these shorter chapters, rather than incorporating them into long chapters with numerous sections, is to make this book easier for you to navigate and revisit. I wholeheartedly implore you, my friend, please resist the urge to succumb to these types of flashy temptations; you know, fool's gold is misleading in appearance. So, endlessly remind yourself of the old saying, "Not all that glitters is gold."

RECAP:

- Profits from trading and investing in leveraged ETFs: Around $12K via day trading.
- Losses from trading and investing in leveraged ETFs: Over $25K via short and mid-term investments.
- The culprit: Lack of knowledge on the topic, lack of discipline around my short- and mid- term investment strategies, and neglecting the importance of setting a stop loss. So, did I learn my lesson? Continue to the next chapter and find out!

POP QUIZ:

Q: Do the math, what was my net trading profit from the leveraged ETFs?
A: $13K in the hole, YIKES!

CHAPTER 10
NFL (NO FREE LUNCH): THE RISK-TAKER

"I had a margin call in 1924 and I swore I never would buy on margin again. That is one of the main reasons I got through the 1930s."

—Philip Carret

Diving headfirst into actionable decisions with little knowledge is dangerous—and trying to make a quick buck with that little knowledge is even worse. "Wisdom is not a product of schooling but of the lifelong attempt to acquire it," said Albert Einstein.

In my efforts to keep learning and advancing my skills beyond day-trading, I developed a basic options trading skillset. Options seemed to me, like they were ten times more profitable than leveraged investments. The greatest advantage being that I always knew my maximum loss would be the price I paid for the option.

There are endless strategies when it comes to trading options. Not to mention, options on leveraged ETFs or volatile stocks have the potential to make 10x profits in just one trade. Can you tell I was on a slippery slope? Surrounded by all sorts of shiny temptations, trading way less, and instead being preoccupied with finding ways to earn megabucks in one fell swoop. I told myself that I was racing against the clock, my sister's necessary medical treatments required money, stat. Desperation infiltrated my trading system/discipline and I was completely unaware of it.

Covered call strategies became my next fixation, they seemed extremely alluring to me. *According to Bank Rate, "A covered call is a kind of options strategy that offers limited return for limited risk. A covered call involves selling a call option on a stock that you already own. By owning the stock, you're "covered" (i.e., protected) if the stock rises and the call option expires in the money. A covered call is one of the lower-risk option strategies and it's even suitable for beginning options investors."* I picked a variety of stocks and looked at their current market price, what their covered call options were worth for the strike price, then did the math and discovered that for every $10K I invested, there was approximately a $2K return on a covered call option. I told myself that the market had not fallen below 10-15% in corrections for many years, so, I'd profit from this mid-term investment strategy.

For example, I bought TQQQ for $50 x 100 = $5,000, and against that, I bought a covered call option of $1,500 for a year ahead. So, if the price of TQQQ continued to rise as it would in a bull market, a year from now, I'd have made $1,500 on that $5K. That is more than a 25% return. Sounds promising, right? In an ideal bull run, I'd have hit a home run on this.

So, I took all my profits from day trading and invested in all the leveraged ETFs with covered calls. It was very exciting, the thought of sitting on a 25-30% return in a year, as long as the market continued to go up. Seems smart, right? The thing is, I didn't stop there, I started to toy with the concept of margin trading with margin money offered by my brokerage account, who were offering to give me roughly $150K with 2% interest. That would mean a 25% return, it seemed too good to be true, but I vetted the terms and it was all legit.

Basically, I forgot that it wasn't technically my money and if margin trading didn't go as planned, I still had to return the money I borrowed. After all, there's no such thing as a free lunch. Well, dabbling in margin trading was the biggest mistake of my life! Never will I ever make that mistake again. If I can prevent just one person, just one of my readers, from blowing it so astronomically, then my job here is done.

After being lured into buying all those covered calls, right at the market's peak, a market dip decided to come on the scene. At first, I watched calmly because I had coverage of almost 30%. These were leveraged 3x, so if the market dipped 10%, the ETFs would dip 30%. Unfortunately, the market dipped way more than 10%, so the ETFs dipped A LOT and before I could even understand what was happening, I was screwed.

Almost every week, I received margin calls, which had me scrambling to transfer the money, in order to rectify the deficiency promptly. When the amount in your margin account drops below the minimum value previously indicated by the broker, you will receive a margin call; alerting you to either deposit cash, transfer in securities, or sell stocks to raise your equity within a few days. Otherwise, the brokerage has the right to sell any securities in the account—or force liquidation. Fortunately, right around that time, one of my real estate properties sold and generated some profit. I immediately sent that over to my broker—nip it in the bud.

Believe it or not, the market dip not end there, I kept telling myself," It's OK, the market will bounce back. This mindset is detrimental, friend, especially with such high-risk mid-term investments. Evidently, my investment strategy was unwise (i.e., no stop losses), things finally declined to a point where I had to break into my emergency fund and immediately transfer all the money to stop the maddening margin calls.

Moral of the story, stay away from margins for eternity, period! I'm in the process of recovering from these losses, but at least now, I'm aware of what my focus and strategy should be going forward.

RECAP:

- Profit from margin trading: Around $25K via day trading.
- Losses from margin trading: Over $75K via short- and mid-term investments.

- The culprit: Lack of knowledge on the topic, lack of discipline around my short- and mid- term investment strategies, and neglecting the importance of setting a stop loss. Most of all, greed; I was consumed by greed.

POP QUIZ:

Q: Do the math, what was my net margin trading profit?
A: Over $50K in the hole.

CHAPTER 11
PARABOLIC FREE FALL: THE GAMBLER

"Behind every consistently profitable trader, there are a lot of losses, mistakes, and lessons learned."

—Unknown

My obsession with "hitting the jackpot" continued to derail me from my learned skills and the practice of my discipline. I started to chase stocks, a scary habit; a quick way to empty your account before you even realize what happened. "Chasing stocks" refers to entering an investment after finding out about a developing trend—in an attempt to rake it in on short-term trends. However, usually, this means you're too late to the party.

Chasing the market is very different from trading stock that has increased in volatility, which you trade with discipline. Becoming a chaser had me buying high at peak price and selling low. On other occasions, I bought stocks high and held onto them, incurring huge losses. As a consequence of my FOMO, I developed this bad habit of randomly picking emergency stocks, not doing any research, and buying it—simply because it had been hyped up on social media. I also bought their associated covered calls, a common strategy to use if you think the underlying price won't move much in the near future. As I'm writing this, I can't help but shake my head because I know how it sounds, A BAD IDEA. But, when greed gets the best of us, it's like pulling the batteries out of your smoke detectors, you can't hear the alarms going off.

If you're only trading to "win big", chances are—you're gambling—and you will neglect to identify a losing trade and get out before it's too late. The four most memorable examples and my biggest chasing mistakes were Upstart (UPST), Coinbase (COIN), Teladoc (TDOC), and Robinhood (HOOD). Without any fundamental analysis, I mindlessly entered long positions on these stocks, with covered calls, and this is what happened:

- UPST: I bought $350 x 100 shares = $35K and sold a covered call. Meaning, I got paid $13K in exchange for giving up a portion of future upside, assuming that in a year UPST would be worth more than $350 and I'd make a $13K profit on my $35K investment. Another big assumption was that if the prices fell, the market would correct by 10 - 15% at the most. So, I covered almost 35%. In other words, even if the stock fell by 35%, I still wouldn't lose. Sounds like a promising theory, right? Too bad I didn't set any stop losses whatsoever. Today, this stock is worth less than $20, over a 90% drop in price, meaning my net $22K investment isn't even worth $2K today, amounting to a huge $20K loss.

- COIN: Similarly, I bought this at around $250 x 100 shares = $25K with a covered call worth over 9K for one to two years apart. Today, that stock is worth less than $50, another major loss.

- TDOC and HOOD: The exact same mistake, yet again, buying high with almost 30% covered, thinking there was no way I could lose, but I made my bed—so I had to lie in it.

The main causes of this disaster:

- Entering investments based on greed, instead of fundamental analysis is a futile endeavor.

- Investing long-term in hyped-up parabolic stocks (stocks with short-term price spikes; often followed by swift downtrends).

- No exit strategy, no plan to limit losses, no way to reduce emotion and risk.

- Betting on a 10-15% market correction in hyped-up parabolic stocks was unsound.
- It can't always be a bull market; we need to prepare for a bear market.
- No discipline defined for selecting long- or short- term investments, asset allocation, or diversification strategy.
- Information overload from social media + purely sentiment-driven = a perfect storm.
- Nearly identical mistakes made as the ones from back in 2000. History repeated itself, which means that regrettably, I hadn't learned from my own mistakes.

Yvan Byeajee, seasoned trader and educator says, "The mind is a fascinating instrument that can make or break you." I learned this lesson in the hardest way possible, losing years' worth of day trading profits, through baseless short-, mid-, and long-term investments. Please, don't fall for the parabolic chase, this is pure gambling. Remember, what goes up, must come down.

Have you heard of the term "Pump and Dump"? It's when scammers flood the internet with false statements; an illegal scheme. First, they "pump" the share prices significantly higher, then they "dump" their shares for an inflated price. It's a con, simple as that. Even so, the market still has these hyped-up parabolic stocks appear almost daily. These schemes only work because of all the sentiment-driven folks chasing momentum. Instead of pursuing "what's new and exciting", we should channel that energy into formations and patterns.

You need to be vigilant, to avoid becoming one of the dumpsters for these pump-and-dumpers. Sadly, ultimately, someone will end up getting duped, which then completes the fraud lifecycle. Always ask yourself this question, "Am I ready to lose what I'm putting in?" These are very well-orchestrated illegal scams; artificially inflating the market price of vulnerable stocks through false promotion, then making prices dip sharply, subject schemers to heavy fines. They know that they're violating a number of federal securities laws, so why do they still do it? (1) Because they think they can get away with it and (2) because people fall for it, period!

Every year, a large number of victims fall prey to financial scams, the root cause being our impatience, greed, emotions, impulses or lack of knowledge—making us vulnerable. The best ways to avoid getting duped are (1) stay up to date with the latest scams, (2) buy yourself time to do research before accepting any offers or making any trades, (3) turn to experts or professionals for guidance, and (4) what Ron Weber said, "If it seems too good to be true, it's probably a fraud."

Once you're disciplined on all levels and become well-versed in technical analysis (to predict the probable future price movement based on market data), then, you may profit from parabolic stocks. However, until you've reached that level, don't even waste your time considering them, unless you're ready to lose it all. Just remember what happened to me and feel free to use this cautionary tale to warn your loved ones too. Also, there's nothing wrong with seeking professional advice about how to protect your family's assets and income.

Not going to lie, I still feel the urge to trade daily or profit daily. I wouldn't be surprised if there's a degree of addiction involved; an addiction to winning, daily. This book not only benefits my readers, but also myself, it serves as a constant reminder to maintain consistency and only enter positions that are supported by my trading discipline. FOLLOW YOUR TRADING SYSTEM, which outlines (1) what, when, and how much to buy; (2) when and how to exit (winning and losing positions); and (3) risk management practices (set stop loss point, set take profit point & never put all your eggs in one basket). You can't win a war without a battle plan, friends.

RECAP:

- Profits from investing in parabolic gambling: Around $15K via day trading.
- Losses from investing in parabolic gambling: Over $50K via short-term or mid-term investments.
- Net trading profits from parabolic gambling: Over $35K in the hole.
- The culprit: Lack of knowledge on the topic, lack of discipline around my short- and mid- term investment strategies, and neglecting the importance of setting a stop loss. Most of all, greed; I was consumed by greed and led by my emotions.

POP QUIZ:

Q: Finish this sentence: Greed is your biggest _________.
A: Enemy!

CHAPTER 12
HOLD ON FOR DEAR LIFE: THE HODLER

"The key to trading success is emotional discipline. If intelligence were the key, there would be a lot more people making money trading... I know this will sound like a cliché, but the single most important reason that people lose money in the financial markets is that they do not cut their losses short."

—Victor Sperandeo

Perhaps a smidge off-topic but significant to my story as a moonlighting trader. I've always been inspired by Warren Buffett's achievements, whose main investment strategy was to buy into companies and hold onto them long-term... In some cases, for life, on account of his belief in the potential of the company. Sounds awesome, right?

What is extremely important for all aspiring traders to be aware of is that the success of utilizing this approach hinges on one's solid knowledge of fundamental analysis. It's not based on "a hunch", it relies on only investing in companies you can easily analyze and are eager to maximize shareholder value, calculating the economic value added (EVA), and even projecting the future owner's earnings. This is all easier said than done, so don't go around operating on a hunch, thinking you're channeling your inner Warren Buffet, ha-ha! What I'm trying to say is, there's more to it than meets the eye, there's a method to the madness of GOATs.

Through a retail traders' group on social media, I learned the term "HODL", which stands for "Hold on for Dear Life". In other words, don't sell it! Originating from the Bitcointalk forum, where an accidental drunken-typo of "hold" appeared. More often used in the crypto world; the general idea is that one should keep holding their coins, even when the price drops or a bear market is on the way.

It seems to pay to be a crypto HODLer—and it also seems pretty easy, right? All you need to do is set up a brokerage account and purchase meaningful stocks, then just HODL. But how do you know whether you're looking at a meaningful investment or a shilling trap? I bet 90% of shilling happens via implicit advertising on social media. This is just another typical pump-and-dump scam, taking advantage of unsuspecting investors. Sometimes "influencers" are also taken advantage of—or they're in on the scheme, promoting something they have a personal stake in.

HODLing is not only the ability to hold on to something for dear life, but also the art of knowing what is worth holding on to for dear life. Pause, read that again. Ok, so, what's my HODLer story? Well, I fell into this trap while following some of these groups on social media that were promoting certain stocks. My instinct was to say, "I just got duped by the wrong ones by accident" or "I just misjudged it because I'm still learning". The truth is, I'd made enough "oopsies" of this sort that it had become a scapegoat for my mistakes.

Excuses are a classic defense mechanism, used to temporarily avoid guilt, shame, and self-blame. Yup, I said it, it's temporary—because eventually, it will all catch up to you. You know how people can go into shock when they're injured? But denial doesn't stop the bleeding, does it? What we need to do is STOP THE BLEEDING! Saying, "Oops! It's ok, I'm ok," doesn't make you ok. Instead, pause, identify the source of the bleeding, apply pressure on it with a sterile gauze until it stops bleeding, then bandage it up. What happens if your bandage is dirty? You may develop a nasty infection. What happens if you don't apply a tourniquet when needed? You may lose a limb. Are you picking up what I'm putting down here, my friend?

That was me, the wounded guy in shock, acting like I was fine and kept trying to move. Sadly, my rock, my mother, was no longer with me to keep me in check and I'd become a loose cannon. Guru, my mentor, was super disappointed in me. I kept this from my sister for a while, until one day, I finally decided to confide in her. Not only did she hold space for me, but also shared so much wisdom with me, it almost felt like my mother was speaking through her.

These chapters discussing leverage, margin and parabolic trading, are examples of me HODLing. Holding on to my investments in new, up and coming IPO companies that were overhyped and not worth my time or money. Nearly 90% of those companies took me on a rollercoaster ride; after entering at the peak and either exiting at the trough or just HODLing. Fooling myself into believing that it would pay someday.

Just like with leverage, margin, and parabolic trading, HODLing can be a profitable method IF you're a disciplined, seasoned trader, who completely knows what they're doing. Otherwise, be prepared to lose it all, especially if you can hear the voice of greed. Remember, only risk what you're ready to lose.

RECAP:

- Profits from HODLing: Around $45K via exiting upon realization.
- Losses from HODLing: Around $100K via holding on because of greed and delusion.
- Net trading profits from HODLing: Over $55K in the hole.

POP QUIZ:

Q: Ok, now that we've done this a few times, what was the culprit?
A: Lack of knowledge on the topic, lack of discipline around my short- and mid- term investment strategies, and neglecting the importance of setting a stop loss. Most of all, greed; I was consumed by greed and led by my emotions.

CHAPTER 13
SIMPLICITY IS BLISS: THE TREE SQUIRREL

"One of the funny things about the stock market is that every time one person buys, another sells, and both think they are astute."

—William Feather

Did you know that tree squirrels are the quintessential biggest hoarders in the animal kingdom? They go through an elaborate process of collecting and storing a wide variety of different foods (i.e., nuts, acorns, seeds, berries, and human food) underground to prepare for the winter. This chapter is about the time Guru called me out for acting like a tree squirrel.

Guru caught a glimpse of the portfolio I was building, using the profits I'd made day trading over the years. He was shocked and said that I owned half of the S&P 500 index share list. "Wait, how could I own almost 250 different company stocks?" I thought. Actually, I had over 150 different company stocks in my portfolio, but that's not all. I had less than ten stocks of each company's, in some cases, only one stock. There were also nearly fifty different company penny stocks, 100 units of each. The quantity probably wasn't the issue, the issue was that my portfolio was PACKED; I was like a tree squirrel with dozens of buried caches.

There was no method to my madness, which led Guru to ask me this question, "Why? What were you thinking?" I had no plausible answer, only a realization, an awakening, that my portfolio needed to be decluttered! I spent an entire weekend determining my portfolio strategy, decided to sell most of what I had, and replace them with ETFs and a few select stocks with good dividends. Also, I created a separate account for my penny stock collection, a.k.a. the "lotto tickets" that I hung on to.

Unintentionally, my portfolio was packed like sardines, congested and distracting! This was the same account I used for day trading, which is a bad idea if you also want to monitor your investment stocks. My "4 to 5" focused day trading discipline had mutated into "14+" AND I was monitoring almost 20 stocks with day trading potential. No wonder I had a hard time focusing, chasing stocks and considering every jump (every opportunity). Not only were my eyes bigger than my appetite but I was also experiencing "the grass is greener on the other side" syndrome, unhappy with my profits because other stocks in my watchlist ran way better that day. Sounds exhausting, doesn't it?

This became the biggest barrier to remaining motivated because my measure for success was no longer whether my method worked, but whether I'd picked the most running active stock from my list. Finally, Guru came over one day and convinced me to create a simple view that had no more than six charts in my watchlist. He helped me appreciate the saying, "Simplicity is bliss." The transition from my tree squirrel trading habits—to a neatly and methodically arranged portfolio—took a couple of weeks. It wasn't easy, but it was so worth it!

RECAP:

- Profits from having the portfolio of a hoarder: I had no clue, it was jam-packed!
- Losses from having the portfolio of a hoarder: Hard to say, I was just glad to decompress my portfolio (and myself)!

POP QUIZ:

Q: What was the culprit?
A: Let's blame "the grass is greener on the other side" syndrome for a change!

CHAPTER 14
SAME SAME BUT DIFFERENT: THE COPYCAT

"Thousands of experts study overbought indicators, head-and-shoulder patterns, put-call ratios, the Fed's policy on money supply... and they cannot predict markets with any useful consistency, any more than the gizzard squeezers could tell the Roman emperors when the Huns would attack."

—Peter Lynch

Sorry to break it to you, but most of my profits earned from day trading (via my awesome tips mentioned in previous chapters), were lost due to my bogus mid- and long-term investment mindset/approach. I'll share more about that later in this book, as it will help you make sensible decisions, fine-tune your reinvestment strategies, and respect/re-invest the profits you earned with blood sweat and tears.

So, after realizing that I'd messed up, again, I became pretty skeptical; and started searching for new and improved ways to become successful. Now, my main methodology and functioning system that I'd built was still there, but I didn't have the patience to continue—because I wanted quick, big wins; that's never a good sign. $25K-$50K per year via a trading side gig was not enticing for me. I got hooked on this traders' group on social media with folks sharing wins from $10K to $100K or more with one single trade. There were dollar signs in my eyes—and I decided to imitate people's trades.

Completely neglecting the fact that I actually had a pretty solid trading system, I began reaching out to people to find out their strategies. I so badly wanted a slice of the pie that they possessed. Introducing: "The Grass is Greener on the Other Side" syndrome!

After reaching out to Guru, asking him to share his daily trades with me, he said, "This is not the way." He was disappointed in me and told me very adamantly that I shouldn't piggyback other people's trades. He said that I should be building my own system; a system that I'm comfortable with and can keep growing from; a system that is made up of my needs, my principal risk level, and my knowledge. In other words, not some cookie cutter plan.

Whoever said, "Patience is a virtue" wasn't kidding… If only I'd stuck to the trading discipline and system that Guru helped me develop, I'd have made enough by now to achieve financial freedom, retire from my day job, and pursue my passion to make a positive impact in the world. Now, when I look back at my system, there were at least a few days every quarter of the year where it could've generated thousands of dollars in just one day. Too bad I didn't have the patience to follow it religiously. All I needed to do was wait for the opportunity to show up and be there when it happened! It was as simple as that, yet I allowed greed and impatience to derail me.

My system showed proven opportunities for me during:

- The US-China trade war (Jul 2018 to Jan 2020)
- The Covid-19 pandemic lockdowns (Mar to May 2020)
- 2021 Stimulus checks (Apr 2020, Dec 2020, and Mar 2021)
- Presidential election (Sep to Nov 2020)
- Vaccine roll-out (Jan to June 2021)
- Russia's war in Ukraine (Began Feb 2020—ongoing now in Jan 2023)
- Global shipping crisis (Began Apr 2021—ongoing now in Jan 2023)
- And many more

Due to doubting my own trading system and only believing in it half-heartedly, I wasn't there or ready when those opportunities presented themselves. I also allowed my fear of losing (immediately after each trade), my greed to only make winning trades, and my extreme reaction to lost trades to completely throw my off-course. The irony doesn't escape me; desiring instant gratification on profitable trades, yet, finding instant losses on unfavorable trades totally insufferable.

In a matter of months, I paid for memberships to several trading platforms and forums, for the sole purpose of copy-trading the positions of these so-called "experts" in the groups. What I learned from those platforms and forums was that these traders were simply sticking to one method of their choice. When the markets were highly volatile, these traders backed the wrong horse more often than not, can you believe it? This was a clear indication that even some of these experts needed to re-calibrate their trading systems; to account for changing market conditions and imminent volatility.

Many factors can contribute to sinking a ship; flooding (through openings in the hull), a collision, loss of stability (also called "roll"), poor weather conditions, human error (negligence), faulty equipment, improper maintenance, or poor planning. Similarly, in a bear market, when fear is prevalent among investors, even a small oversight can sink your "ship". This is why it's absolutely critical to fine-tune your trading system BEFORE the storm hits, my friend. Believe it or not, a trader who is on the ball, may even use volatility-induced market dips to generate profits.

Not going to lie, it seemed to me like many of the members on those platforms were high-frequency traders. You know how red-bellied piranhas, who have razor-sharp teeth, super strong jaws, and usually hunt in groups? Did you also know that when one of them smells blood, he'll signal his buddies to attack, triggering a feeding frenzy, stripping the prey down to the bone in minutes, then peace out? This is what those traders were like, I'm not kidding. Imagine an innocent fish, maybe an endangered bocachico, arrives late to the party—so he has NOTHING TO EAT. You guys, he's already endangered and now, not only will he probably starve to death, he may also absorb contaminants from the water and sediments. Poor bocachico… Please don't be like this bocachico, ok, friend?

Today, I stand corrected. Guru was right to scold me about trying to be a brainless copycat and instructing me to avoid paying for several memberships to those copy-trading platforms. The good old "teach a man to fish vs. give a man a fish" logic, am I right?

RECAP:

- Profit from copy-trading: Around $2K via selling upon realization.
- Losses from copy-trading: Around $8K primarily via swinging options
- Net profit from copy-trading: Over $6K in losses.
- The culprit: Come on, it's right under your nose—closet copycat!

CHAPTER 15
LACK OF KNOWLEDGE: OPTIONS, OPTIONS, OPTIONS

"I have been trading for decades, and I am still standing. I have seen a lot of traders come and go. They have a system or a program that works in some specific environments and fails in others. In contrast, my strategy is dynamic and ever-evolving. I constantly learn and change."

—Thomas Busby

Trading options is experiencing exponential growth, because they are full of possibilities. Basically, these are contracts that allow buyers to buy ("call") or sell ("put") the underlying asset at a specific price on or before expiration. I don't plan to go into detail about options in this book; options are a simple yet complex topic. I'll save that for a different book, if and when I get to it. There's a lot of information out there on YouTube if you want to learn more about options.

If you jump into this without proper knowledge of how to carefully weigh the risk, you can lose your entire principal in a blink of an eye. In my opinion, options are equally as risky as parabolic stocks. However, if one can master options, there's the potential to make decent profits with small capital.

When trading options, I suffered major setbacks and also noticed many folks losing six figures or more (on a social networking platform for traders that I followed closely). Many people posted about their huge losses from trading options. Approximately 70% of my losses are attributed to options. Remember the chapter where I mentioned covered calls? Not only did I think that I was buying into a safety net, without a good grasp of how options work, I also lacked in-depth understanding of the market. You have the world at your fingertips; instant access to information and strategies. Just remember, you need to be super disciplined and good with numbers. Options trading requires extensive research, developing a battle plan and sticking to it. Nobody ever won a war by "winging it".

The first time I got into options, I joined an online trading group, a service that shared daily options to trade. I'd imitate their trades and it went well, initially, but as the market became volatile, most of their trades went south—and so did mine. Herd mentality is no joke, friends. Without individual analysis, we're all just sitting ducks. Finally, I canceled my subscription to that trading group.

The second time I tackled options, I decided to understand and carefully study every options trade that Guru had ever executed. He graciously agreed to continue sharing his options trades of the day for me to analyze and learn from. Wanting to be a good student, I also watched numerous videos online (about options trading). First came cognitive overload; my brain was trying to process too much information—but I kept diving deeper, then, came clarity.

With my newfound knowledge, I decided to try out covered calls, meaning I sold someone else the right to purchase shares of a stock that I owned ("covered"), at a specified price ("strike price"), at any time on or before the expiration date. Then, well, you already know how the rest of that story goes. If I attribute 20% of my options losses to that subscription service, then I attribute 80% of options losses to my covered calls.

Finally, I admitted that it was time to pause, re-evaluate and re-establish my option trading discipline. You know, although options were the cause of 70% of my losses, they were also the reason I bounced back, after taking control of my trading. Sharing is caring so here is what I did to gain much-needed focus:

1. Every step of my trading system, detailed in earlier chapters.
2. Instead of stocks, I only traded same-week or same-day expiry options.
3. TQQQ or QQQ were the only options I traded (and still are)!

That's it! I hope this helps you fully comprehend the importance of pausing, decluttering, and rearranging everything into an organized system. Systemize your portfolio, your life, AND your mind! Because simplicity truly is bliss, my friend.

RECAP:

- Profits from options trading with herd mentality: 40% of all my profits; and that's just the beginning!
- Losses from options trading with herd mentality: 70% of all my losses; but when one door closes, another one opens!

POP QUIZ:

Q: What was the culprit?
A: ME! I was to blame and I am to be famed!

CHAPTER 16
FOMO AND FUD: THE SCAREDY-CAT

"Trading is not for the dabblers, the dreamers, or the desperate. It requires, above all, one steadfast trait—dedication. So, if you are going to trade, trade like you mean it!"

—Rod Casilli

The past few chapters are classic examples of the kind of chaos that fear infused with greed is capable of breeding. Every chapter exposes a substantial trait or weakness that stands in the way of you becoming a successful trader. We were all born with the "fight, flight or freeze" response, a survival mechanism that was designed to help us react quickly to life threatening situations.

We were designed to FREEZE and play dead when approached by certain animals, FIGHT like hell when attacked by certain animals, and FLIGHT—run for your life when chased by certain animals. What would've happened to cavemen who mixed up their responses? Well, they would've gotten eaten, bro! So, what do we do when our caveman brains take control? If only our brains could be programmed like automated software, so we'd always react to threats perfectly and systematically. Am I right?

According to CFI, "The Fear and Greed Index, developed by CNNMoney, is used to gauge whether investors are too bullish or bearish on the stock market. The index ranges from 0 (extreme fear) to 100 (extreme greed)." Wait a minute, did I just say that the pros created an actual tool to literally gauge investor sentiment, also known as human emotions?! Yup, that's how predictable our caveman brains are, my friends. The good news is, there's a way to hack this evolutionary adaptation with—you guessed it—discipline!

Listen, a study published in the International Journal of Paleopathology, looked at cortisol accumulation in the hair of 2,000-year-old Peruvian mummies and found "repeat exposure to stress". Just because those mummies were stressed from having to figure out everything about hunting, gathering, and surviving without Google—doesn't mean we have to be like them! These sentiments are one of the key reasons why 95% of traders haven't achieved success yet.

Fun fact: (1) Koalas will fight and bite each other over one eucalyptus leaf; which they have to work hard to digest because they're poisonous! (2) Sloths sometimes mistake one of their own limbs for a tree branch, slip, and die! (3) Turkeys are mesmerized by rain and can stare with their mouths open until they drown! (4) Pandas have a meat-eaters digestive system, yet they insist on chewing on bamboo all day! (5) Ostriches, like toddlers playing hide-and-seek, when they push their heads against the ground, they think they're invisible to predators. Thankfully, we aren't like these stupid creatures…right? Say yes.

We are, however, predisposed to herd behavior (a.k.a. FOMO—fear of missing out). According to Psych Central, researchers discovered that it takes a minority of just 5% to influence a crowd's direction—and that the other 95% follow without realizing it. There was a time when this instinctual behavior would've evolutionarily helped humans survive, but nowadays—our innate desire to follow the herd, can offset our discipline. Don't forget, we are also capable of independence and self-reliance! Discover the beauty of JOMO (Joy of Missing Out) and maintain control over your decision-making.

Let's talk about JOMO, the joy of missing out, this will be your stepping stone to disciplined trading. Ingrain this into your brain:

- JOMO is the best way to counteract FOMO!

- JOMO is intentionally choosing what to keep and what to give. This is a step toward determination—and with determination comes discipline.

- JOMO is wisely choosing to ignore fads like Jordan's, Gucci, Louis Vuitton, Audi, Ferrari, Lamborghini, and I guess FOMO stocks. "I Have Spoken."—Kuiil

- JOMO helps you frame the moment and focus on the bigger picture, which fosters gradual progress. With incremental growth, comes the prospect of exponential growth!

- JOMO is the art of getting better results through a "simplicity is bliss" lens. This helps you unpack your brain and remove distractions. In other words, it brings much-needed focus. Become a "minimalist-trader". Taking up minimalist-trading will help you rewire your trading discipline into a simple and effective system. The best thing is, this applies to all areas of life.

As you learned in this book, it took me a while to reach this level of autonomy. But when I finally did, I started to feel so much lighter and even noticed that there was a lot more time for myself, which is how I found time to write this book. Now, my trading system looks a lot more decluttered compared to before. Whenever you find yourself off the JOMO track, view that as a "scheduled maintenance message", reminding you to pause and recenter yourself.

What FOMO traps have I gotten myself into?

- IPO FOMO: When I wanted to buy into almost every new company that was getting listed on the stock exchange. Primarily due to the urge to follow the herd (with no fundamentals).

- Long-term FOMO: When I noticed people holding on to certain stocks solely out of emotion, I did it too (because I didn't want to miss out on what the herd was doing).

- Quick money FOMO: Several chapters in this book speak for themselves. Classic case of FOMO.

They say there are 5 stages of grief, I say there are 9 stages of FOMO:

- Pre-FOMO "FUD": I'd watch trades and not enter, due to my own fear, uncertainty, and doubt (created by yours truly).

- Stage 0—Feeling great: The herd convinced me to get over my FUD.

- Stage 1—Time to buy: I entered the FOMO cycle. No fundamentals, not realizing how close I was to the parabolic roller coaster, and ignoring the risks of the downside.

- Stage 2—Super positive sentiment: I saw it further going up and forgetting it had reached the peak. This is the classic greed stage with the highest risk. I wanted to hold on for more profits. Discipline had already been enslaved by FOMO.

- Stage 3—The first slide: Here we go! Prices dropped and money lost!

- Stage 4—Denial: After losing over 20%, I was still hopeful that it was just a correction and would soon go up.

- Stage 5—Panic selling: Suddenly drops more than 70%; I watched helplessly, regretting not taking the profits and not cutting the losses. Big mistake.

- Stage 6— Baseless HODLing: Don't want to sell or buy the dip, so I HODL with the hope that someday, there will be another FOMO ride for me to get my money back. I say "baseless" because over 90% of the time, these parabolic FOMO stocks will only have one run and be done. I'd even look at a dead cat bounce with hope and HODL! *According to CMC Markets, "A dead cat bounce is a bearish continuation pattern. When the stock price is dropping, the price rises temporarily but then resumes its downward trajectory."*

- Stage 7—The realization: "One day that stock will only be worth a few cents, after dropping over 99% in price, and going through several reverse splits. In some cases, companies will get delisted or file for bankruptcy. Oh my god…"

- Stage 8—Bargaining: The herd is moving again; I need to get in there and avenge my past losses! (Inner monologue: "This time, I won't make the same mistake… this stock isn't the same.")

- Stage 9—The wake-up call: It took me incurring an almost six-figure loss to wake the hell up. Let me tell you, it wasn't easy to be out of the fantasy (or addiction) and feeling left out.

Learn from my mistakes and avoid this trap like the plague, my friend. It's taken a lot more time and effort for me to bounce back than if I'd had my wake-up call after stage 3, 4, 5, 6, or 7. I certainly would be ballin' by now if I'd stuck to my trading discipline this whole time!

A note on FUD: There are several instances in the market, when FUD is used as a tactic to drive a bullish sentiment away from the herd, which would result in a change in trends or periods of extreme volatility. This is a tactic that's used to drive market corrections, a bearish sentiment, or FOMO. That's how it goes; FUD is a propaganda tactic, used in sales, marketing, public relations, and even politics. The best way to combat FUD is via TFYS; Think for Yourself! No, I'm not telling you to go dig for conspiracies. TFYS entails: (1) Honing your craft. (2) Deepening your understanding of stock charts and market data. (3) Improve your ability to find accurate information, interpret data quickly, and decipher market activity.

RECAP:

- Profits from being a scaredy cat trader: Six-figures, on paper.
- Losses from being a scaredy cat trader: Six-figures of my real money
- Net from being a scaredy cat trader: This book!

POP QUIZ:

Q: What is the prerequisite for TFYS (Think for Yourself)?
A: Digital literacy! This entails:
(1) Effectively gather, evaluate, and use information.
(2) Use critical thinking skills to plan and conduct research, manage projects, solve problems, and make informed decisions.
(3) Practice legal and ethical behavior online.
(4) A sound understanding of technology concepts, systems, and operations.
(5) Please, I beg you, as a human in the 21st century, perfect these crucial skills!

CHAPTER 17
FEAR OF LOSING & GREED FOR MORE: THE PREDICTOR

"The function of economic forecasting is to make astrology look respectable."

—John Kenneth Galbraith

After several setbacks with my short-term investing strategies and losing significant amounts of money, I built a fear of losing, which pushed me to build discipline. On the other hand, my greed started calling the shots; it was telling me to invest an entire day's profits into high-risk stocks and options. It happens; mistakes are a part of life. Learning from failures is how most achieve success!

Not setting stop-loss levels as a part of my high-risk investment strategy—was the biggest mistake. The "I'll get it back someday" mindset was also detrimental. I'm not talking about 10% or 20% losses; I'm talking about over 90% losses on some big investments I made in those parabolic high-risk stocks. When John Cena said, "If you don't learn from your mistakes, they become regrets," he wasn't kidding. If a person makes a mistake and immediately learns their lesson, that's acquired wisdom, my friend! If a person repeats the same mistake, even after knowing it's a mistake, that's just straight up ludicrous—and this is me being nice.

This type of foolish, unreasonable, stubbornness is dangerous. If not timely addressed, significant trading losses often lead to both emotional distress and turmoil— which may cause flashbacks or anxiety in future trades. So, I urge you, don't be like me. Or maybe I should say, don't be a turkey! Don't be a sloth! To really get the point across, ha-ha. Please, take these lessons and remain disciplined by reminding yourself of the cautionary tale about Shiv. This is the only way!

Those losses hit me hard, my emotions convinced me that I was no good at trading. My brain completely overlooked the fact that I was doing fine day trading and swing trading; the problem was my aggressive investment strategy, diving headfirst into high-risk stocks, filling up my portfolio with high-risk and volatile stocks, with no stop-loss or discipline! When you list it all out like that, it sounds really bad, doesn't it? That's why you need to learn how to think critically BEFORE you make a decision, not after shit hits the fan!

Feeling like a huge loser, I became an overly-cautious trader, started to hesitate to enter any trade, and overanalyzed every little thing. Years of profits, hard work and discipline wasted, just like that, all while my emotions were bubbling over. Just to clarify, being meticulous and diligent is good, being anxious and fearful is not. The looming worry of "what if…" and "am I wrong?" consumed me. I was constantly nervous about losing money; it felt like I was drowning from over-thinking and I could hardly keep my head above water.

My belief in a functioning trading system was shattered—and there was no one around to tell me that I wasn't thinking straight. You know what marathon runners say to each other? "Stay in the moment, don't write the review of your race before it's over." I love that. This is exactly why when a trade doesn't go in your favor, you should: (1) Close your eyes and take three slow deep breaths while telling yourself, "I will breathe through the frustration. I'm allowed to feel disappointed. Adapting is my superpower. This too shall pass; I'm going to be ok. (2) After you've calmed down, figure out why and how things went wrong. (3) Recognize that this is akin to mile 18 of a marathon; it's traumatizing, painful, and you feel like you might die. You have 5 seconds to decide if this is where you (A) hit a wall or (B) trust your training, stay on course, and eventually cross the finish line. I'd choose B, how about you?

Feeling like I was practically back to square one, I stopped trading and decided I'd rather watch and predict the market. After nearly reaching a 90% (consistently 80%) accuracy, I started to feel like some kind of "market seer" who could prophesy stock moves. However, along with that ability—came regret. Yup, you guessed it, hello FOMO my old friend...

Turns out my FUD was even stronger than my FOMO at the time. Although Guru was receiving texts from me containing my predictions of the market (we used to keep score of our accuracy), I was still frozen and terrified of losing any more money. It was so bad that even on a confident prediction day, if I somehow managed to enter a trade, I'd exit and take a $10 profit, just to be safe.

This "exit at $10" behavior had me acting like a guerilla trader; move in, take $10-25 and quickly move out. One day, Guru stopped by my place and I showed him some of these trades, he painfully watched my miserable state and told me, "You need to rebuild your life and your portfolio, because it's not over yet." Although I heard and understood what he was saying, my confidence was nowhere to be found and I was simply not ready to lose again. To be honest, a little piece of me knew that I could bounce back, but I just was nowhere near ready yet. Healing takes time, my friend, and that's ok. Surprisingly, I ended up making $4000 via guerilla trading, without even realizing.

One day, I called my sister and decided to come clean about the financial losses I'd incurred. No, you're not experiencing déjà vu, this is something I also mentioned doing in Chapter 12 (after HODLing), ha-ha. So, not only did my sister listen to me, she was also super chill about it. Instead of focusing on my losses, she responded by reminding me of (1) all the things I'd learned over those few years, (2) my biggest assets—the skills I'd developed, and (3) how far I'd come. Her wisdom was therapeutic, that discussion was more effective than any 3 or 7 day "detox", I walked out of there feeling lighter. After a few weeks of regularly chatting with my sister, I began to feel more like myself again. She even joked, "Think of it like an expensive tuition fee you paid the stock market, in exchange for a master's degree in Trading Discipline."

As my amygdala chilled out and my "freeze" mechanism faded, I was able to pragmatically tell myself, "Yes, I did lose over six figures. Yes, that is undoubtedly a huge amount of money. Yes, especially after working my ass off trying to contribute to my sister's cause. Yes, this loss is a huge setback for us both—BUT—it's not the end of the world. This is not how my story ends."

Fun fact: right before I messed up and lost a bunch of money from investing in high-risk stocks, my sister actually mentioned, on a call, that she felt I should refrain from any type of "gambling." Without knowing that I'd already doubled my high-risk investments, she tried to warn me, probably because she could sense my greed and impatience bubbling over. Well, being a classic little brother, sitting on over 100% in profits, I ignored her warning. In my super confident mind, I was convinced that this was not gambling, I thought I was investing smarter than Warren Buffett! "Everything is based on analytics!"

If I'd listened to my sister instead of ignoring her, I would've doubled my investments. A word of advice, if you have a wise older sibling, friend, or family member who's almost always right, maybe don't let your "hotheaded little brother" persona take the wheel. On the bright side, if I had listened to her, this book probably wouldn't exist!

Public Apology: Sorry, sister, for losing the funds I tried so hard to build for your cause… Thank you for your unconditional love and forgiveness. I hope to make you proud someday!

CHAPTER 18
I HAVE A GUT FEELING: THE INTUITIVE

"If you want insights that can make you more money, look at the scars running up and down your account statements. Stop doing what is harming you and your results will get better. It is a mathematical certainty!"

—Kurt Capra

As my sister gradually diffused my guilt of the previous financial loss (caused by my mistakes), I started to regain confidence in myself and my trading discipline. This was revolutionary. Remember how I kind of became a Guerrilla trader—and unintentionally generated almost $4000 in profits over a couple of months? Well, it turns out that most of those techniques were just an effective trading pattern.

Here's what I mean:

- In order to curb my fear of losing during a live trade, I started by trading small.
- I reduced my incurred losses on a trade to the cost of going out for dinner.
- On days that I had to cut losses, I'd make myself food at home, instead of ordering takeout. I'm not kidding, that is how I justified my losses. That was the power of fear that originated from my painful financial loss. Thank God I am finally out of it, but it sure took a lot of convincing (myself) to resume trading again. I started scalping, executing multiple trades, whenever it felt right. *According to CFI, "Scalping is a day trading technique where an investor buys and sells an individual stock multiple times throughout the same day. The goal of a scalper is not to*

make an enormous profit with each individual trade they make, but rather to make a small profit over many little trades. Effective scalpers must be able to read and interpret short-term charts. They must often make decisions based on stock charting that is within 1 to 5-minute intervals."

- I began allowing my intuition to decide whether or not to take a trade. Now you know why there's an entire chapter dedicated to the intuitive!

This intuition was not something that I just randomly developed—or some kind of mystical sixth sense I was born with. Upon deeper reflection, I realized that it was built, piece by piece, over years of observing my effective trading system until it became second nature.

Perhaps you've previously heard of intuitive trading. I promise you that this is doable, all you need to do is practice your trading system—and then practice some more. With consistency, you're on your way to successfully becoming an intuitive trader too! Once you've mastered this, it'll be like riding a bike. You just need to learn how to "see through the matrix" first. PSA to Gen Z: if you haven't watched one of the movies that defined a generation, do it now, don't walk, run.

CHAPTER 19
OPTIMISM IS A SUPERPOWER: THE HOPEFUL

"We must accept finite disappointment, but never lose infinite hope."

—Martin Luther King, Jr.

You know, Jim Cramer, host of Mad Money on CNBC and an anchor on Squawk on the Street, tells people that, "Hope is a bogus emotion that only costs you money." But I disagree. In my opinion, hope is never a bogus emotion; what costs me money is greed. Greed of quick money, HODLing, missing out on a slice of the pie, losing "the game", and instant gratification. Greed often disguises itself in various forms, such as delusional, unjustifiable, false hope.

Hope—is what saved me. Hope gave me the power to overcome greed and clear the fog. Hope is the fuel of humanity; it's everything. It can reduce stress and feelings of helplessness, increase happiness and quality of life. It was hope that generated courage; so that I could conquer the mental health challenges I experienced, triggered by my mother's passing and my sister's illness. Like world Zen master, Thich Nhat Hanh says, "Hope is important because it can make the present moment less difficult to bear. If we believe that tomorrow will be better, we can bear a hardship today."

March 2021 to March 2022 was by far the hardest time in my life to date. First, my mother "graduated from Earth school", then, my sister fought for her life. I was beyond overwhelmed and it showed. My mental and physical health hit rock bottom. For most of 2021, I felt so disoriented. Not only did I totally lose interest in my passion for trading stocks and crypto on the side, but it also felt like I'd lost my purpose in life. Due to my grief, I couldn't even think straight. This kind of fragility was so new to me; someone who became "the man of the house", after my father passed away, as a clueless—but hopeful—17-year-old boy. In my culture, sons are expected to pick up the responsibilities of their late fathers, thankfully mine had raised me well those first 17 years of my life.

As a teenager and young adult, my hope was built on the belief that I just had to do my best and the Universe would take care of me. Have you ever noticed how children just seem to have faith in people and the world? They believe the best in people and the world. You may call that gullible, I call it profound. But somewhere along the line, we lose that and become cynical or disconnected from real people and the real world. Wouldn't the world be a better place if we weren't all in such a hurry to tuck away our inner child? Wouldn't the world be a better place if we all stayed young at heart and let our inner child out to play?

Regardless of what you may think, this is all pertinent. Continue to walk alongside me and you'll see… sometimes all we need is a listening ear or a shoulder to lean on when times are tough. I was fortunate to receive this type of solace from my sisters, friends and chosen-family, Utkarsh, Ashok, Kaushik, Ella, Alice, and many more including Guru. They, along with their families, were my support, until I was ready to take over again. Not to mention, my amazing manager's support was like finding a sturdy, floating buoy amidst a thunderstorm at sea. I'm endlessly grateful for their compassion.

As mentioned in earlier chapters, time passed, my overall health improved, and I resumed my day job. I still had no interest in doing anything else and the search for my purpose in life continued; however, listening in on my day job's 1-2 conference calls per month (with the company's CEO) began to pique my interest. The CEO's motivational talks not only reignited hope within me, but he also chose topics that inadvertently seeded my cause and purpose in my life, bit by bit. My CEO unknowingly became my hope giver and, in a way, helped guide me towards finding my "ikigai" (the concept mentioned in Chapter 8). He even dedicated one week for all employees within the organization to participate in "the Week of Equity and Action". His inspiring speeches, his passion to make a difference in the community, and his hope was contagious. He had a flair for creating a company culture that embodied his core values; empathy, giving back to the community, and serving others. This really fueled my hope and encouraged me to align my life with my "ikigai", my reason for being.

Some may have called that a mid-life crisis, ha-ha! Thankfully, I can laugh about it now. As you've already read in previous chapters, in late 2021, some irrational decisions were made when attempting to resume moonlighting trading. I was back to doing it half-heartedly (again), unsure of my career calling (again), allowing greed and emotions to cost me money big-time (again). Moral of this particular segment of my story? If you don't break a bad habit, its cycle continues. Just like good habits can be automated, so can bad ones.

According to award-winning New York Times bestseller and Pulitzer Prize–winning journalist, Charles Duhigg, the only way to short-circuit the habitual pattern is to identify the cue, the routine, and the reward they deliver:

> Step 1: Identify your habit loop: Figure out the routine, the reward, and the cue. The routine is the bad habit you want to get rid of, for example, dining out too often. We all know how quickly an appetizer, main course, dessert, and maybe a drink, can add up. The reward is feeling more sociable and fun or to relieve stress (temporarily). The cue is feeling too tired to cook or wanting something to look forward to.

Step 2: Experiment with rewards: This stage can last days, weeks, or months; like a scientist collecting data, this is when you'll experiment with different rewards. Remember, awareness is half the battle! So, on a day that you feel the urge to ask your colleagues out for dinner, instead, invite them over for a movie and freshly made popcorn! On a day that you feel the urge to meet your buddies at a sports bar, invite them out for a swim or game of basketball and bring a homemade smoothie or coffee! The next time, make time to prepare an epic post-workout meal for you to enjoy after the gym. The next time, invite a friend on a hike and pack some gourmet sandwiches. The next time, try out a meal service; either one that brings you "meal kits" with simple recipes to follow or one that delivers 3-5 healthy, affordable, chef-prepared meals for your fridge. And so on, and so forth—this is how you rewire your brain and redesign the habit!

Step 3: Isolate the cue: Remember, awareness is half the battle. Challenge your cravings by asking questions. Are you wanting to dine out because you're already starving and your fridge is empty? Do you want to go out because you feel like celebrating? Are you wanting to dine out because you haven't done any meal prep? Identifying cues will allow you to see the patterns. According to Healthline, experiments have shown that almost all habitual cues fit into one of five categories: (A) Location (B) Time (C) Emotional State (D) People Around You (E) Last Action. Every time you're tempted to repeat the bad habit, write down the location, time, emotional state, people around you, and your last action. Soon, it will be clear which cue is triggering your bad habit.

Step 4: Have a plan: Once you've identified all three components of your habit loop, it's time to make a plan to rewire your brain! Remember, awareness is half the battle! The only way to get rid of a bad habit (created via repetition) is to replace it with a good one (created via repetition). Don't beat yourself up if you're not perfect, an "all or nothing" mentality only gives people excuses to quit. Instead, trust the process and keep going until it becomes automatic!

In early 2022, I resumed trading (moonlighting). A lot had changed; I was less attentive, leaving some investments unwatched. Some grew while some blew—and I missed out on some major market trends. It didn't help that market sentiment had switched from extreme greed to extreme fear, hype, or uncertainty. It was a whole new world. Bulls were being chased out by the fear of bears; bears were becoming territorial and bulls were losing ground.

It was time to dust off my day trading knowledge, tools, skills, and plan. Before I jumped back into trading, I watched the market like a hawk, conducted a self-inventory, looked back on my last 4+ years of trading, and clearly perceived that I was a different person. Definitely a better version of myself, who now approached everything with purpose—which inspired me to write this book. You, my reader and friend, kept me accountable.

While not everything "happens for a reason", I do believe that we all have the ability to make something sweet out of something bitter. I'm thankful that the Universe carried me through my disastrous performance and led me here. I'm thankful for the opportunity to turn my story into a "survival guide" for novices, advanced beginners, and competent returnees who are looking to rewire their trading—and avoid my impressive compilation of mistakes. Also, I wanted to show you via this book that disciplined trading works. "This is the way!" —The Armorer (The Mandalorian)

A solid "belief" system does not have glitches. In other words, no baseless beliefs. They can sneak up on you and before you even realize, they're already in charge. This is why we need to be realistic, be logical, use our knowledge, and continuously assess ourselves. Self-inventory is vital to ensure we haven't strayed or fallen into any "belief traps". These traps derail us from our trading discipline and, as you know, cost me big-time. Some of the most hilarious, bizarre, and just plain stupid belief traps I've fallen for:

- A couple of times, I bought into day trading Tesla stocks out of emotion instead of using my trading discipline. Guess what? Each time I did that, I incurred losses. I had to cut losses and run out of the trade with my tail between my legs. At long last, my belief system was strong enough to see that trading Tesla always cost me. The Truth: Each time I traded Tesla, I didn't follow my trading basics.

- "If I trade Amazon, I will always profit." I believed this to the extent that, at times, I'd randomly scalp Amazon with no fear, without even thinking about my rules. The Truth: I'd simply developed a strong intuition for entering Amazon trades, built through years of discipline and experience trading Amazon stock.

- "I don't like the word SPY, so I'm never going to trade SPY." Yes, really. I wish I was kidding. The Truth: I can't even. Let's just leave it at that.

- "I shouldn't trade any cigarette stocks." The Truth: There's nothing wrong with setting standards or boundaries around which stocks to invest in. We all have our own lifestyle preferences.

- Holding on to losing Tesla stocks just to make my point; that I needed to break my superstition that Tesla stocks fell whenever I'd purchase. The Truth: This is just straight up passive-aggressive! Don't fight the market, my friend, pick your battles! Instead of being headstrong like this, make an entry using a solid trading system!

- "My sister warned me against gambling, I should've listened to her." The Truth: I got derailed from my trading discipline and, yes, that was sheer gambling. That type of behavior and mentality is dangerous anytime, whether my sister warns me or not. After that, I stepped up my game by exiting gambling with stocks, followed a trading discipline, and forever remembered to listen to my sister instead.

Take control of your belief system, my friend. Never let false beliefs enter your system and steal your focus. We are sentimental, emotional beings who constantly require self-inventory. Make it a practice to assess yourself regularly; monthly or even bi-weekly. Evaluate your trades, emotional state, progress and measurable goals. If needed, seek help from someone you trust. If you want to be in this for the long haul, you're going to need motivation and commitment. This is what we'll discuss in the next chapter.

CHAPTER 20
MOTIVATION & DRIVE: THE COMMITTER

"Most people fail not because of a lack of desire but because of a lack of commitment."

—Vince Lombardi

According to the Cambridge Dictionary, "Motivation" is the willingness to do something—or something that causes willingness and "drive" in a planned effort to achieve something." Both of these things are indispensable factors for success in trading. You must find your motivation, commit to your drive, and create a game plan. What is your trading goal? How are you going to achieve it? Without accountability or a catalyst, we can lose our pep! This is hardwired human nature, my friend. At my day job, I'm extremely result-oriented, because I'm accountable to deliver! Working for yourself can be tricky, so you'll need to apply some productivity hacks.

How to fuel motivation: Figure out what lights a fire under you. Without a purpose, you have nowhere to go, how sad is that? Identify something that gets you out of bed in the morning. Set milestones that you can reach and celebrate. Find an accountability-buddy who can support you (and vice versa) to keep commitments and maintain progress. Can you think of anyone? Hey, if you don't try, you'll never know!

Ideally, you can find an accountability-buddy or mentor within your everyday life; someone you can regularly meet with, text, and call. Let me ask you: Who do you know that has similar goals and ambitions as you? Who do you look up to—in your existing network? The idea is: during your regular "check-ins", you'd both evaluate your progress and whether or not you stuck to your discipline. This is the path to habit formation, building consistency, and increasing maintaining accountability. Some unicorns—I mean people—are extremely driven and self-aware, unlike the rest of us normies. As you must know by now, I'm extremely grateful for my mentor, Guru, who shared all his wisdom with me so generously. If only it hadn't taken me five years to learn my lesson.

My commitment to write this book was inspired by seeing so many people making the same mistakes as I did—losing their hard-earned money. Not to mention, all the stories about people suffering from mental health challenges brought on by financial hardships or relationship issues. Worst of all, the news of folks who lost their lives to depression—after going bankrupt and being in major debt.

Life is so incredibly precious. It is a privilege to be able to wake up every day and walk the earth. Whether you believe it or not, we were all put in this world for a purpose. We must make it our mission to leave this place a little better than we found it. Agatha Christie once said, "Just to be alive is a grand thing." So how do we cherish this gift? Take care of your physical and mental health—attentively.

My sister suffers from persistent, long-standing pain, stemming from her chronic health conditions. She is a perfect example of someone who values life; despite needing help every day, she never stops fighting. If you're looking for a purpose in life, my sister will welcome you (literally with open arms) to join her cause. If you don't know what your dream is yet, feel free to help her fulfill her dream of setting up emergency shelters for the elderly and disabled folks experiencing homelessness. Have a chat with my sister and you will learn to appreciate your blessings.

The craft of "discipline" is endlessly preached in this book, which of course had me constantly reminding myself, "You can't just talk the talk, you've got to walk the walk." So, I carried out a self-inventory on my mind, found it stuffed with experience and acquired wisdom, and decided that it was time to unpack all the goodies for my fellow humans. You, my friend, get to benefit from this journey I've gone on—to excavate and deconstruct every single piece of useful knowledge in my mind.

This has not been an easy journey; in a world that seeks instant gratification, writing this book has not provided quick rewards or recognition. However, I had the motivation to produce something valuable for you all—and my drive to reach people with this book as soon as possible, helped me stick to my commitment. If I can prevent one person from experiencing financial ruin or a mental breakdown, then it'll be worth it. Journaling not only uncovered my strengths and weaknesses, but also helped me hone in on my trading skills. Now, I implore you to do the same, find your motivation and drive, develop a game plan so you can stick to your commitments. I believe in you, friend.

CHAPTER 21
TRADING WITH PATIENCE: THE FISHERMAN

"Investing in yourself is the best thing you can do, and as a part of investing in yourself; you should learn more about money management."

—Warren Buffett

Would you like to be the bait or the fisherman who uses the bait to frequently catch small fish—and periodically bring in big fish? Avoid being tempted by the shiny apple; there are a lot of sharks out there, sitting with their mouths wide open, my friend. I made that mistake, time and time again, and walked straight into it. Thankfully, the shark bait I carried with me, allowed me to free myself from the trap and escape, this may not be the case for others. So, I urge you to resist the impulse of falling for those bait traps. Remember, there are faint clues in the water that caution smart fishermen to avoid becoming the bait. Similarly, there are tiny signs in the market that alert a smart trader to avoid falling in the trap and becoming the bait. As Thomas Jefferson once said, "Do not bite at the bait of pleasure, till you know there's no hook beneath it."

In my opinion, every time I made the mistake of falling for the trap, the culprit was my inner desire to experience the high of raking in money overnight. In pursuit of this guilty pleasure, I failed to spot the snare underneath. Subconsciously, I knew the risks. I knew I was making dicey bets. What I didn't know was that all those bets would tank. The main reason I was able to climb out of that hole, is my dominant nature of being risk averse. This core trait of mine ensured that despite sustaining a six-figure loss, I still managed to bounce back from it.

This would be a suitable place to insert a giant yellow "CAUTION" sign, because not everyone finds a way to recover from such a tough blow, which is why we should never risk more than we can afford to lose. This is vital. Read that again and again, until it's ingrained in your brain forever. Let me repeat that, "Never ever risk anything that you're not ready to lose." Transform your mind so it's as sharp as a steel trap. I paid a hefty price for my mistake and didn't have expendable cash left to make the best out of the market volatility. I had to restore my finances before I could return to trading—a lot better prepared. This is when I thought of another quote of Warren Buffet's, "Be fearful when others are greedy and greedy when others are fearful."

Trading in the market with the right techniques are skills that need to be garnered. If you want to catch tiny fish, stay in the shallow water. If you want to catch big fish, you've got to dig deep; that's where the buried treasures are. Yes, precious gems are mesmerizing. Yes, shiny gold is irresistible. Only, are you prepared for this? Are you equipped with the right gear? What are the conditions of this dive? Do you have any surface support? How motivated are you? Are you ready for this, mentally and physically? Because you don't want to run out of air down there.

When deep diving, your risks of running low on air and nitrogen narcosis increase as you go deeper, but these risks are manageable with ample training, the right equipment, experience and a carefully considered plan. This is exactly how you should approach partaking in the stock market. As a beginner "diver," you should stay above 60 feet. Give yourself time to internalize skills and procedures at a comfortable depth. Ensure that you're completely comfortable with shallow diving before you go deeper. Deep diving is considered anything below 100 feet and carries its own set of risks and rewards. However, any pro will tell you that the key is to train in baby steps.

Once I was able to recommit myself, determined to resume moonlighting as a trader, I took the approach of a prosperous fisherman. Before I share more details about how I approached my trading, let's think about what makes a successful fisherman. No, I am not here to teach how to fish but this is truly the perfect metaphor for trading.

Let's compare the attributes that fishermen and traders possess which contribute to their success. There are many different reasons people like to fish. Some do it for the appeal of the scenic excursions, while others do it for the thrill of the sport. Some do it as a hobby, while others do it as an income source. The same goes for traders. You need to know why you're doing it. If you're trading just as a hobby for a social excitement or for a thrill, I'd recommend knowing your limits (of how much you want to spend trading). I say "spend" because most likely you won't be disciplined in the skill to profit.

Some of the key skills required to be a skilled fisherman involves:

- Patience: Fishing requires patience and persistence, so does trading. Fishing is a sport of trial and error, so is trading. Patience with perseverance is the key.
- Reading the Water: This is an art; reading the surface of water to determine where the fish may be. Ripples, color changes, standing rips, and visible structure are some of the key characteristics to look for in finding fish. Similarly, trading is an art; reading the market trends to determine where the good trades may be. The market also has observable characteristics that we need to look for, this is when our trading systems come in handy.
- Casting: The difference between catching a fish or missing it, is a matter of having the correct grip on the fishing rod, this makes the casting more effective. The same goes for trading on the market, you must learn the art of having the

correct grip on your trading system, this makes the trades more effective.

- Stealth: Have you ever played hide-n-seek in your childhood? Remember how quiet we had to be? When fishing, the more we limit our noise, the higher the chances of catching fish without scaring them away. When it comes to trading, limit the noise in your mind and quiet your emotions. With an undisturbed mind, you will catch the right, profitable trades.

- Reeling: Another skill that (finally) brings the fish into your hands. When to reel, how to reel, when to stop, when to let go, and when to wait; all things you should know during this process. The same goes for trading— when to enter, when to exit, when to take profit, when to cut losses, and when to wait. These are the essential factors you should be aware of, otherwise you'll never be able to reel in your profits.

- Baiting: Having the right bait is crucial; fish can be easily lured by live bait. This is where traders need to be extremely aware when entering a trade. They shouldn't be drawn to just any bait dangling in front of them. With an effective trading system and discipline, you'll never fall for decoy bait, no matter how luring or enticing it may appear.

- Determination: Success in fishing is a combination of research, practice, trial and error, and sometimes pure luck. Not only do you have to be patient enough to learn and develop your skills, but you also need to have the determination to see it through. It's easy enough to come up with a plan before you hit the water but sticking with it and not giving up when the fish are not biting is how you truly become a good fisherman and catch that trophy fish. May I suggest that you read the determination point again? And in doing so, simply replace fishing with trading and replace fish with trade. You will be amazed at these interchangeable traits of fishing and trading. "This is the way!"

- Adventurous: If you want to succeed at fishing in the long run, you need to be willing to take chances and make changes. Going to the same spot, using the same equipment, and trying for the same fish every time will get boring and, eventually, leave you coming up dry. You must be eager to try new places, techniques, species, and technology to break up the monotony and keep growing your abilities. With trading as well, there will be times of lull and if you reach that point, recalibrate your trading system. The key is you should be willing to take chances and make changes when things are not working out.

- Education: If you want to catch some fish, you can't just pick up a pole and head to any body of water you'd like. You need to research the species you're targeting, the best locations to go, conditions of the water, anticipated weather, new tactics to try, and the latest equipment available, among many other things. The more you know about fishing, the better fisherman you will be. Do you catch my drift? Apply this to your trading mindset; your trading system needs to be equipped enough, enabling you to do the required research. No matter how mechanical your trading system is, there's a set of steps you need to consistently follow as part of your discipline. That is education!

I developed these qualities mentioned above as I resumed trading. I decided to stay focused only on TQQQ for a long time; I only took TQQQ trades, nothing else. I primarily went for their options or stocks. I stayed focused and patiently read TQQQ trends and analyzed stock charts. I kept my mind as calm as I could and started to rebuild my trading system. Those consistent small wins accumulated over $4000 in profits. Whenever I entered with my bait, I was ready to reel it in, utilizing my trading system protocols. I remained educated and determined. After continued success, I started feeling a little more adventurous, exploring futures trading, and relying on my tried-and-true trading system. *According to Nerd Wallet, "A futures market is an exchange where investors can buy and sell futures contracts. In typical futures contracts, one party agrees to buy a given quantity of securities or a commodity, and take delivery on a certain date. The selling party to the contract agrees to provide it."*

This is just the beginning for me; it took me almost six years to get here! Before I end this chapter, I must clarify—I'm not actually into fishing. So please don't go around hurting innocent fish all over the world just to practice stock trading. This was a chapter full of analogies, not coercion to go participate in the overfishing industry and habitat destruction. Please don't get me wrong!

CHAPTER 22
BACK TO BASICS: THE SAILOR

"We search through historical data looking for anomalous patterns that we would not expect to occur at random."

—Jim Simons

Let me tell you something about sailors, people usually have the belief that a good sailor is one who knows how to be calm under duress. However, according to the American Sailing Association, beyond that, "Good sailors are usually just calm in general." So, how do they do it? The ASA says that it requires a combination of solid understanding of fundamentals, experience (a.k.a. practice), calmness (a.k.a. noise cancellation mode and clarity), and intuition. Sound familiar?

By now, I'm sure that you no longer require me to spell out how those same skills will benefit you in trading. On the other hand, what do they mean by "intuition"? Well, Dr. Ann Sloan Devlin, Professor of Psychology in New London says, "Sailing is a very analytical sport; it certainly exercises your brain in a way that other sports don't. You think a lot, it's not always just 'feeling' the boat." I've got to ask again, sound familiar? Now you know why I found the similarities between the skills of surfers, fisherman, and sailors to be so inspirational!

Let's expand on these analogies. In theory, surfer-traders and fisherman-traders will consistently profit and always take steps towards achieving financial freedom. For many, this is good enough, these folks are blessed with the quality of contentment. Most surfers and fishermen prefer not to stray too far from land. However, sailors love to explore the world and discover new land! Skilled sailors achieve this through ample practice and experience, accumulated over time. Similarly, a sailor-trader is someone who can sail through any market condition, navigate the choppy stock market sea—and become a standout explorer!

In my opinion, my "trading level" resembles the skills of a seasoned surfer. I evolved from a fisherman—and while I'm content with my progress, I wouldn't mind becoming a great maritime explorer-sailor. Whether I've evolved into a maritime explorer-sailor or not, won't be gauged by how many miles I've traveled or how much gold I possess. Instead, it will be weighed by how many people I connected with and how many lives I had a positive impact on during my quests.

It hasn't been easy, thankfully, the approach of disciplined, gradual progress has been vital for me. My original vision of achieving financial freedom and retiring rich has shapeshifted into achieving incremental success. Not that we shouldn't have an end goal in mind, but like Drake says, "Sometimes the journey teaches you a lot about your destination."

Since recovering from the financial-hit I took, due to the derailment of my disciplined trading habits, I've come a long way. I've been preparing extensively and gearing up to sail into uncharted waters of the market in the coming months. It won't be an easy voyage, but I'll have all my years of experience (with trial-and-error) at my fingertips!

I'm holding out hope that you'll become a fellow sailor and join me on an expedition one day. In order for that to happen, you should know that (in addition to "solid understanding of fundamentals, experience, calmness and intuition) the ASA also indicated the following qualities of a good sailor:

- "Jack of all trades: The ability to think on your feet and improvise is the quality of a good sailor. There's nothing so comforting as being around good sailors who, when faced with a problem, simply start figuring out solutions based on the materials on hand."

- “A boat is a boat: Someone who really knows how to sail can hop on any boat and make it hum. He or she will do a quick inventory of how the particular systems on the boat operate and in a matter of minutes will be an integrated crew member or skipper working as if they have been on the boat for years.”

Let me add these as well:

- Tacking: A maneuver that allows you to sail in the desired direction.

- Enjoy life: Make time for the things that bring you joy.

- Give back: Sailors contribute to society! (Fun fact: according to Marine Insight, “90% of the world's food, fuel, raw material and manufactured goods are delivered by sea. Nearly all things sold worldwide are transported through ships, which need skilled seafarers to operate, maintain and repair.”)

- Mental toughness: This means they won't crumble in the face of adversity.

- Dedication: This means that they’re totally committed to their mission and willing to do whatever it takes to see it through.

This is precisely the kind of sailor-trader that we should aspire to be. What’s also notable: good sailors have a love for the sea, they’re there for the right reasons—because the ocean is a part of them, not because they want to find a shortcut to some mythical treasure—or escape reality. Good traders must enter the stock market for the right reasons and value their own money. Good sailors respect the ocean; they’re humble, not arrogant, in the face of nature—and acknowledge that nature is all-powerful. Good traders are not arrogant, they respect market trends and sentiment.

Good sailors are detail-oriented and methodical—following a systematic, established procedure—and so are good traders!

Check this out: Sailors who stay focused on their tasks are able to avoid most mistakes, just like us traders with our metaphorical "noise canceling headphones" on. This also means, when sailors drop the ball, it's going to hurt! Meaning, they will learn the hard way, just like us traders when we take a financial hit. Ok, let's end this chapter with some quotes that are as good as gold:

- "Ships don't sink because of the water around them; ships sink because of the water that gets in them. Don't let what's happening around you get inside you and weigh you down." —Unknown
- "If you are going to do something, do it now. Tomorrow is too late." —Pete Goss, a British yachtsman who has sailed more than 250,000 nautical miles.
- "Sailors, with their built-in sense of order, service, and discipline, should really be running the world." —Nicholas Monsarrat, Lieutenant Commander and British novelist known for his sea stories.
- "To reach a port we must sail. Sail, not tie at anchor. Sail, not drift." —Franklin D. Roosevelt
- The wind and the waves are always on the side of the ablest navigator. —Edmund Gibbon, English historian, writer, and member of parliament.
- The pessimist complains about the wind; the optimist expects it to change; the realist adjusts the sails. —William Arthur Ward, American motivational writer.
- "A ship in the harbor is safe, but that's not what ships are built for." —John Augustus Shedd, American author and instructor.

- “It is not the ship so much as the skillful sailing that assures the prosperous voyage.” —George William Curtis
- “Failure is only the opportunity more intelligently to begin again.” —Henry Ford, American industrialist, founder of the Ford Motor Company.
- “Don’t listen to what they say. Go see.” —Ancient Chinese Proverb
- “There is nothing noble in being superior to some other man. The true nobility is in being superior to your previous self.” —Ancient Indian Proverb
- “The future depends on what we do in the present.” —Mahatma Gandhi

CHAPTER 23
INSIDE THE MATRIX: CRACKING THE CODE

"Before you can inspire with emotion, you must be swamped with it yourself. Before you can move their tears, your own must flow. To convince them, you must yourself, believe."

—Winston Churchill

There's always another opportunity-train for you to hop on, so please don't allow regret to consume you. Guilt and shame will only waste your time and energy—and cause you to miss the next opportunity-train. 24-7-365, there's an infinite flow of opportunities sent our way in the trading market. It's not an exaggeration to say that there's an opportunity every second of the matrix—I mean—stock market.

Are your reasons for day trading or swing trading as clear as crystal? How will you make the most of the time you dedicate to trading? Time is money, my friend. Some prefer to be a short-term or long-term investor; some choose to be a dividend earner; while others elect to be a day trader or swing trader. Every trader has reasons for choosing their trading style. If you're still searching for yours, I'm sure that with some research and/or maybe future blog posts by me on Rewired.guru (pending availability), you'll be able to find a strategy that best suits you. Keep in mind, I am not a financial advisor though.

In trading, your opponents are other traders—and digitized information processing systems. You must rewire your brain, in order to harness the power of a free mind. When playing chess against computers, you can only go so far. Instead, learn the laws of physics within the Matrix, one level at a time. When playing against humans, well, I just think of this quote by Jesse Livermore (a pioneer of day trading): "Wall Street never changes, the pockets change, the suckers change, the stocks change, but Wall Street never changes, because human nature never changes.” Not to mention, this quote by Bernard Baruch, (an American financier who made a fortune on the New York Stock Exchange): "As a student of human nature, I always have felt that a good speculator should be able to tell what a man will do with his money before he does it."

Michael Burry, an American investor, hedge fund manager and physician once said, "It is my belief that one constant in the stock market is human nature." That’s what I think of when I look at penny stocks and meme stocks. *According to Investopedia: “A penny stock refers to a small company's stock that typically trades for less than $5 per share. Meme stocks arose in the year 2020 out of the subreddit r/wallstreetbets; they are so-named because ideas about them, too (like memes), spread rapidly online on social media and web forums. Meme stocks also see communities built around them that perpetuate the hype and elaborate on the original meme, inventing specific terminology and symbols to accompany the stock.”* Careful; at times, machines will allow us humans to be led by our emotions, before taking over and wiping out all these humans’ cash.

10 lines of code to hack the trading matrix (transcribed from Investopedia):

```
<div id="myDIV" class="header">
 <h2>My Trading Matrix Script</h2>
 <input type="text" id="myInput" placeholder="Title...">

<span onclick="newElement()" class="addBtn">Add</span
>
</div>
<ul id="myUL">
```

<li> 1. Always Use a Trading Plan: A trading plan is a written set of rules that specifies a trader's entry, exit, and money management criteria for every purchase. With today's technology, it's easy to test a trading idea before risking real money. Known as back-testing, this practice allows you to apply your trading idea using historical data and determine if it's viable. Once a plan has been developed and back-testing shows good results, the plan can be used in real trading. **</li>**

<li class="checked"> 2. Treat trading like a business: To be successful, you must approach trading as a full- or part-time business, not as a hobby or a job. If it's approached as a hobby, there's no real commitment to learning. If it's a job, it can be frustrating because there's no regular paycheck. Trading is a business and incurs expenses, losses, taxes, uncertainty, stress, and risk. As a trader, you're essentially a small business owner and you must research and strategize to maximize your business's potential. **</li>**

<li> 3. Use Technology to Your Advantage: Trading is a competitive business. It's safe to assume that the person sitting on the other side of a trade is taking full advantage of all of the available technology. Charting platforms give traders an infinite variety of ways to view and analyze the markets. Back-testing an idea using historical data prevents costly missteps. Getting market updates via smartphone allows us to monitor trades anywhere. Technology that we take for granted, like a high-speed internet connection, can greatly increase trading performance. Using technology to your advantage, and keeping current with new products, can be fun and rewarding in trading. **</li>**

<li> 4. Protect Your Trading Capital: Saving enough money to fund a trading account takes a great deal of time and effort. It can be even more difficult if you have to do it twice. It's important to note that protecting your trading capital is not synonymous with never experiencing a losing trade. All traders have losing trades. Protecting capital entails not taking unnecessary risks and doing everything you can to preserve your trading business. **</li>**

<li> 5. Become a Student of the Markets: Think of it as continuing education. Traders need to remain focused on learning more each day. It's important to remember that understanding the markets, and all of their intricacies, is an ongoing, lifelong process. Hard research allows traders to understand the facts, like what the different economic reports mean. Focus and observation allow traders to sharpen their instincts and learn the nuances. World politics, news events, economic trends—even the weather—all have an impact on the markets. The market environment is dynamic. The more traders understand the past and current markets, the better prepared they are to face the future. </li>

<li> 6. Risk Only What You Can Afford to Lose: Before you start using real cash, make sure that all of the money in that trading account is truly expendable. If it's not, the trader should keep saving until it is. Money in a trading account should not be allocated for the kids' college tuition or paying the mortgage. Traders must never allow themselves to think they are simply borrowing money from these other important obligations. Losing money is traumatic enough. It's even more so if it is capital that should have never been risked in the first place. </li>

<li> 7. Develop a Methodology Based on Facts: Taking the time to develop a sound trading methodology is worth the effort. It may be tempting to believe in the "so easy it's like printing money" trading scams that are prevalent on the internet. But facts, not emotions or hope, should be the inspiration behind developing a trading plan. Traders who are not in a hurry to learn typically have an easier time sifting through all of the information available on the internet. Consider this: if you were to start a new career, more than likely you would need to study at a college or university for at least a year or two before you were qualified to even apply for a position in the new field. Learning how to trade demands at least the same amount of time and fact-driven research and study. </li>

<li> 8. Always Use a Stop Loss: A stop loss is a predetermined amount of risk that a trader is willing to accept with each trade.

The stop loss can be a dollar amount or percentage, but either way, it limits the trader's exposure during a trade. Using a stop loss can take some of the stress out of trading since we know that we will only lose X amount on any given trade. Not having a stop loss is bad practice, even if it leads to a winning trade. Exiting with a stop loss, and therefore having a losing trade, is still good trading if it falls within the trading plan's rules. The ideal is to exit all trades with a profit, but that is not realistic. Using a protective stop loss helps ensure that losses and risks are limited. **</li>**

<li> 9. Know When to Stop Trading: There are two reasons to stop trading: an ineffective trading plan, and an ineffective trader. An ineffective trading plan shows much greater losses than were anticipated in historical testing. That happens. Markets may have changed, or volatility may have lessened. For whatever reason, the trading plan simply is not performing as expected. Stay unemotional and businesslike. It's time to re-evaluate the trading plan and make a few changes or to start over with a new trading plan. An unsuccessful trading plan is a problem that needs to be solved. It’s not necessarily the end of the trading business. An ineffective trader is one who makes a trading plan but is unable to follow it. External stress, poor habits, and lack of physical activity can all contribute to this problem. A trader who is not in peak condition for trading should consider taking a break. After any difficulties and challenges have been dealt with, the trader can return to business. **</li>**

<li> 10. Keep Trading in Perspective: Stay focused on the big picture when trading. A losing trade should not surprise us; it's a part of trading. A winning trade is just one step along the path to a profitable business. It’s the cumulative profits that make a difference. Once a trader accepts wins and losses as part of the business, emotions will have less of an effect on trading performance. That is not to say that we cannot be excited about a particularly fruitful trade, but we must keep in mind that a losing trade is never far off. Setting realistic goals is an essential part of keeping trading in perspective. Your business should earn a reasonable return in a reasonable amount of time. If you expect to be a multi-millionaire by Tuesday, you're setting yourself up for failure. **</li>**

<li> Conclusion: Understanding the importance of each of these trading rules, and how they work together, can help a trader establish a viable trading business. Trading is hard work, and traders who have the discipline and patience to follow these rules can increase their odds of success in a very competitive arena. **</li>**

</ul>

CHAPTER 24
ENTER THE SIM: THE PRO GAMER

"Confidence is not 'I will profit on this trade.' Confidence is 'I will be fine if I don't profit from this trade.'"

—Yvan Byeajee

One of the biggest things I struggled with when it came to entering a trade was the fear of an instant, negative outcome. Executing a trade and seeing a profit within a few minutes to a couple of hours is great, who doesn't love instant gratification? However, my challenge was coping with instant loss after a trade went south. Like you, I'm just a commoner, working hard all day just to pay my dues. This is why watching a couple hours' worth of pay disappear in a matter of minutes was unbearable for me. This was a huge hurdle for me; even with a solid trading system and plan, I still struggled to execute trades at the right time.

One thing I know for sure is that I'm not alone in this, there are definitely others like me out there. Thankfully, I found several ways to overcome that struggle. One method I used: each day, never risk more than 10% of what I earned from my day job that day. That was my threshold. On top of that, on the days that I did end up losing that 10%, I'd tell myself, "I hope this money lands in the hands of someone who will do good things with this money. Or even better, one of my friends or readers are profiting from my loss." That really softened the blow.

Remember when we discussed how creating a strong belief system can give you strength? Similarly, a false belief system can completely erode everything you've built. This is why it's so crucial for you to develop a belief system that strengthens you instead of weakens you. This is what I did by rewiring my brain to perceive losses differently. This technique of reframing your thoughts and beliefs is applicable to all areas of your life; even if this particular example of me hesitating to enter trades doesn't resonate with you. Remember, we all have different strengths and weaknesses, so tailor these particular tips here to your needs.

Another method I used to overcome my hesitation: as an avid gamer who used to spend hundreds of dollars on computer games, I decided to rewire my brain to view trading as a sim. For each action that I'd execute in this sim, I'd either win points or lose points; each time I'd break the rules, I'd get a penalty. Instead of, "How much am I profiting or losing?" it was "How do I stick to the rules, avoid penalties, and win more battles than I lose?"

Rules: (1) Too many penalties means game over. Users only need to focus on themselves, there are no opponents as this is not a competition. (2) Hitting 10% in losses means time to review previous moves and re-evaluate strategy. (3) Hitting 20% in losses means a half-time break; time to stop, get up from chair, step away from desk, reduce eye strain and mental fatigue, and move body to increase blood flow to brain. (4) Don't go back in until the frustration meter has been reset and the battle plan has been updated. If needed, seek a second opinion or extra knowledge to help you level up.

Similarly, if your points are positive (10-20% or more), keep going—and as you gain experience, you'll begin to discover patterns and optimal strategies for different scenarios. Remaining calm, positive, curious and viewing losses as lessons learned. This is the key to mastery. However, refusing to step away when you're "tilted" (a frustrated or angry gamer) may worsen your performance and lead to a losing streak. Take a break until you're ready and excited to enter the sim again. Obviously, I'd never endorse treating trading like a game. This chapter exists for the purpose of sharing how I overcame something that I seriously struggled with—and call attention to the fact that you can also rewire your brain to overcome something that you're seriously struggling with. "I have spoken!" —The Kuiil (The Mandalorian)

There was a time when I played chess against computers; it was so therapeutic. Whenever I was exhausted, I'd turn on my computer and play chess against machines, haha! Eventually I mastered 5 out of 10 levels, if I remember correctly. On several occasions, I attempted to advance to the 6th level, but just couldn't beat the computer. Instead of getting tilted, I repeated the 5th level over and over again and learned almost every move the computer would make. One day, I finally decided to try the 6th level again and, to my surprise, I won!

Trading in the markets is like playing against machines. I'd even go as far as to say, it's like being inside the matrix. Fortunately, slowly but surely, one can conquer the matrix by developing endurance, matrix vision, strength, speed, phasing (or adaptation), and precognition (or awareness). Just keep practicing; repetition is the key to mastery.

A pro gamer understands the importance of:

- Self-awareness.
- Being content with their wins.
- Being present in the moment.
- Recognizing their privilege (to be able to do what they do).
- Only competing with themselves, not others.
- Stress management; stress relief.
- Physical health: sleep, nutrition, exercise.
- Self-care (physical, mental, and social).
- Have fun and enjoy the process.

CHAPTER 25
WHO YOU ARE: THE TRAITS

"If I have positions going against me, I get right out; if they are going for me, I keep them. Risk control is the most important thing in trading. If you have a losing position that is making you uncomfortable, the solution is quite simple: Get out, because you can always get back in."

—Paul Tudor Jones

It seems, in this book, I've gone in all sorts of directions talking about my traits over the years. This is the beauty of being human, we go through phases and evolve many times over the course of our lives. As long as those traits make us grow into better humans, that's all that matters.

By now, you're probably dying to ask me, "So, Shiv, have you fully recovered from the two six-figure losses yet?" Well, thanks to my trusty trading plan, I'm over halfway there! And I can't wait to see what the Universe has in store for me!

Anyone who says that they can easily recover from losses of this magnitude, within a few weeks or months, is way too uppity to be associated with us, ha-ha! All jokes aside, I hope you read and recognize that my losses were caused by impulsively taking my day trading profits and throwing it all into high-risk investments. So, basically, gambling; a.k.a. YOU CAN AVOID THIS!

The formula I used to rewire my traits:

- Always stick to my core trading discipline (see Chapter 4: Surfers vs. Traders and Chapter 7: The Resurgent).
- Avoid market distractions that trigger FOMO or FUD.

- Believe what my trading system is telling me when trading; ignore market noise.

- When faced with losing streaks, first, I will evaluate my discipline and adjust my trading strategies as needed (or according to emerging market demands). I'll remember that from time to time, recalibrating the trading system is required—but I will always stick to my unchanging trading discipline!

- Occasionally, when there are lower-risk opportunities with super high rewards, I will take a leap of faith. I will always enter a trade fully cognizant that whatever money I put in may never come back. For example: I invest in over 50 penny stocks and will only cash out if they grow more than 10-fold, otherwise, they're a lost cause to me.

- Once in a while, when the markets or particular stocks are extremely volatile, I'll take those bets. With a clear understanding whatever money I put has low risk but high rewards. Example: Whenever the market drops over 5% or spikes over 5%, I look for low-risk option calls or puts opportunities. I let them run till the date of expiry. Usually, I profit 5 times or it goes to 0.

- From time to time, when there's a strong analytical reason to HODL a given stock, I'll either HODL until I have earned a 20x return or until it becomes 0 (with a clear understanding that what I am HODLing may have 0 intrinsic value a day from now, a week from now, or year from now).

- Never gamble, bet or HODL more than 5% of my total capitals in a given year.

- Give back 10% of my profits on a monthly basis and volunteer towards good causes.

- Keep evaluating myself each month and recalibrating to turn my weaknesses into strengths.

- If I find myself struggling, I'll seek guidance, take a break, spend quality time with family, get some nature therapy, or go out and pay it forward.
- We are all deserving of rest and rejuvenation. I'll make time to recharge.

And there you have it. I can confidently say this, 10 years from now—or 50 years from now—no matter what the trading strategies are, as long as one adheres to their trading discipline, they will never be defeated. I hope it's evident to you by now, that the learnings in this book are not just trading skills but also life skills meant to be passed on from generation to generation.

At the end of this book, I've included a self-inventory questionnaire for you to conduct a (likely overdue) self-assessment. The ability to recognize your temperament, strengths and weaknesses is an invaluable asset. The only way we can turn our weaknesses into strengths is by identifying them, diving deep into examining them, coming up with an action plan (to avoid the "procrastination doom loop") and do the work. There's no shortcut to this.

After self-introspection, if you discover that you struggle to stick to the plan because you're not in it for the right reasons or you're simply not passionate about this kind of stuff—sit with it—then, choose your path. Not everyone is born to be a trader nor can one be forced into becoming a disciplined trader. Listen to your gut. It was Aristotle who said, "Pleasure in the job puts perfection in the work."

Writer Caroline Donofrio shares a helpful framework for honing your intuition, given to her by her therapist friend, Brenda, "When it comes to making decisions, I always ask myself: Does it feel expansive or contractive?" (An idea that was introduced by life coach Marie Forleo) Caroline Donofrio explains, "'Expansiveness' feels light, powerful, exciting. To me, it's like the sensation you get after a workout or when you're "in the zone" doing something you love. When you can't wait to get started on something, there's a good chance you're feeling expansive. 'Contractive' feelings exist at the other end of the spectrum—heavy, tight. Perhaps it carries with it a sense of dread or secrecy. You can also sense it physically—are you hunched over? Is your jaw clenched? Do you feel like you're stuck in molasses? If so, your intuition may be telling you it's a no."

Yes, trading is a "gold mine" that could bring a lifetime of financial freedom, for those who are willing to invest the time, effort, and capital towards getting the hang of it. However, it's easier said than done. Just like underground miners, drillers, blasters, and mine engineers, their work requires an abundance of discipline, patience, focus, passion, and determination. So, look in the mirror and ask yourself, "Is this for me?" and "Am I truly ready?" If you need help, please don't hesitate to reach out! Life and trading coaching is my jam!

CHAPTER 26
MINDFULNESS MEDITATION: THE VISUALIZER

"It's not what we do once in a while that shapes our lives, but what we do consistently."

—Tony Robbins

So, one of the most helpful tools that some brokerage firms have is "Paper Trading". If you don't know what paper trading is, YOU'RE BUSTED! If you skipped through chapters on account of impatience, how are you going to hack it as a trader (when patience is vital for success)? Every section and chapter in this book contains a story and a lesson. If you miss something, not only will you be unable to string the narrative together, but you also risk making the same mistakes I did and get your ass handed to you!

Back to paper trading; much like training wheels, this allows you to familiarize yourself with the actions and concepts involved in trading. Meaning, you get to avoid flying down a hill, crashing, and incurring a road rash—or even worse, a severe concussion. I impatiently skipped the paper trading part, look how well that went for me! So, SMARTEN UP and take full advantage of paper trading, take your trading system for a spin—more like 1-3 months' worth of spins.

Another spectacular tool suitable for daily use, that will definitely come in handy, improve your cognition, counteract stress, boost memory, regulate emotions—a.k.a. STICK TO YOUR TRADING DISCIPLINE—is meditation. Now that meditation and mindfulness is the fastest growing health trend in the world, I'm sure you've heard of it somewhere or other. So, why has meditation's popularity increased so dramatically over the past decade? It could be that preliminary research shows that meditation has been associated with reduced amygdala reactivity (the amygdala activates the "fight or flight" response). Or—it could be that neuroscientists like Sara W. Lazar, PhD, have found that long-term meditators have: (1) Enhanced senses (more gray matter in the auditory and sensory cortex). (2) Better working memories and decision making (more gray matter in the frontal cortex). (3) Improved risk-reward analysis, pain threshold, and empathy (more gray matter in the insula). Pretty cool, right?

On top of that, I also practice visualization to maximize my brain's potential. Did you know that visualization not only taps into underutilized parts of your brain, but brain scans have shown that envisioning yourself doing something activates your motor cortex (the same part of your brain that lights up when you're actually moving)? According to the Sport Journal and Tokyo University of Agriculture and Technology, motor imagery training (or mental practice) can enhance both injury and stroke rehabilitation! How cool is that?!

My visualization technique: Envision my trade entry strategy. Envision my charts. Envision my entry points. Envision exit points (profit taking and stop losses). Envision a smooth, unemotional execution. This mental practice has led me to a point where I no longer hesitate to take profits or cut losses when a trade reaches my defined thresholds. It's no different than the way that athletes use visualization to enhance training, performance, rehabilitation, and mental strength. I think it's safe to say that mindfulness, meditation, and visualization are indispensable life skills for all. Visualize a better you, a kinder you, a more thoughtful you, a more successful you, etc.

Once you've developed the mindfulness techniques mentioned above, you'll be well-prepared to step into the shoes of successful you and better human you. Laugh at me all you want—for visualizing even while sitting in front of my computer; preparing to trade, setting my intentions to stick to the plan and don't forget to breathe (ha-ha). Don't knock it 'till you try it! You'll be amazed by the smooth sailing. If mastered, eventually, you may be able to be done trading for the day in 15 minutes—like me (sometimes)!

Don't forget, our brains are complex. We may use touch, vision, or auditory learning to process and retain information—so why not cover all the bases? We should not be limited to one learning style as our brains possess remarkable cognitive capacity! This is why aside from practice (touch), market research (vision), and visualizing (vision), I'm also a big fan of auditory learning. Speaking and listening is a very effective way to rewire your brain, to enhance critical thinking, comprehension skills, problem solving, and memory. This can mean anything from verbally rehearsing the steps in your trading plan out loud (at least once a day—in the morning) to listening to the Trading Anthem while you shower or get ready in the morning. "What's a Trading Anthem, Shiv?" You ask? Do not fret, my friend, I have attached the lyrics and details on my Trading Anthem for you in the bonus chapter!

Visual meditation tips from me to you:

First, a disclaimer: Individual results may vary. Meditation is not a substitute for therapy or medication. Recommended for individuals with sound mental health. If you have mental health issues, please consult your mental health physician before experimenting with meditation.

1. Find a quiet space: Visual meditation is best done in a comfortable, quiet place with no distractions; a peaceful environment where you can focus on the images in your mind.

2. Set an intention: As you begin, set your intention. What would you like to achieve? This could include clarity of thought, greater self-awareness, inner peace, calmness, or simply allowing

yourself to be open to whatever comes up. You may choose to set a trading intention.

3. Breathe deeply: Take several deep breaths before you begin and be mindful to keep breathing throughout the visualization. This will help you to stay grounded and focused on the images in your mind.

4. Use all five senses: Make your visualizations as real as possible by incorporating sound, smell, taste, and physical sensations along with sight when creating your visualization.

5. Release expectations: Visual meditation is a process of exploration, not an achievement. No need to control the visualization or become too attached to the outcome, rather, be open to whatever comes up in your mind. Just like trading without fear or worry about the outcome; only sticking to your trading discipline.

6. Stay present: Pay attention to your thoughts, feelings, and sensations without judgment or resistance. Stay in the present moment and let the images come and go without trying to alter them in any way. Being present while trading is also key.

By following these tips, you can practice visual meditation more effectively and beneficially. With patience and practice, you may find that visual meditation can be a powerful tool for relaxation, focus, mental resilience, positivity, creativity, and energy boost.

CHAPTER 27
TRADING SKILLS TO LIFE SKILLS: THE HUMANITARIAN

"Use me, God. Show me how to take who I am, who I want to be, and what I can do, and use it for a purpose greater than myself."

—Martin Luther King Jr.

As we develop our trading discipline, we should also work towards becoming better humans. My hope is that we won't spend our lives only chasing superficial goals. May we pursue meaningful goals that not only enrich our own lives but also the lives of others. Just like LOTR actor Viggo Mortensen said, "Life is short and the older you get, the more you feel it. Indeed, the shorter it is. People lose their capacity to walk, run, travel, think, and experience life. I realize how important it is to use the time I have."

As you know, one of my goals is to fulfill my sister's dream—and this book is a small step towards her noble cause. I am endlessly inspired by my sister, a phenomenal mentor, always taking every opportunity to help others, and selflessly dedicating her life to her family. On top of that, she loves mother nature deeply and has a strong desire to care for mother Earth. As you can see, I think the world of my sister, who has suffered so much yet always gives so cheerfully. My Personal Mantra: "It's time for me to repay my sister for her sacrifices and unconditional love."

One thing I've started to do is anonymously donate to causes close to my heart. You should try it sometime, it truly doesn't matter how much you give, what matters is your intention. If you're presented with an opportunity to help someone, take it. I know this is a book about trading, however, my commitment to give back to the world is a huge motivation for me. Every day, it pushes me to keep going and continues to hold me accountable.

This pledge helped me become more consistent with taking profits from my trades in a timely manner; so I can use a percentage to try and make a difference in this world. In the back of my mind is the message, "This money is not only yours, so please avoid dicey or volatile trades—the more you make, the more of an impact you can make." See, giving also rewires our trading!

Desmond Tutu once said, "Do your little bit of good where you are; it's those little bits of good put together that overwhelm the world." I hope you (my dear readers and friends) and I can leave this world better than we found it. I hope that you never doubt that you were put here for a purpose. I hope you never forget your calling. When in doubt, just remember what Mahatma Gandhi once said, "The best way to find yourself is to lose yourself in the service of others." I seriously couldn't agree more. This extraordinary human, who was widely recognized as one of the twentieth century's greatest activists also said, "The true measure of any society can be found in how it treats its most vulnerable members." Oof.

I'm sure you've heard the saying, "Do good for others, it will come back in unexpected ways." Well, this is a tried-and-true formula for me, friends. At times, disciplined trading can begin to feel very mechanical—or even, day I say, boring. That's why you need to have the drive; without it, you're like a car driving on an empty tank. Just like running on empty can damage your fuel pump, living without a cause can lead to burnout.

How to refuel yourself and others:

- Everyone has something they can contribute to the world. Like Mother Theresa once said, "Never be so busy as not to think of others." So, volunteer what you can, whether it's your time and effort or resources.

- To do good for one human, is to do good for the entire human race. Charlie Chaplin once said, "We think too much and feel too little. More than machinery, we need humanity; more than cleverness, we need kindness and gentleness. Without these qualities, life will be violent and all will be lost."

- "The best investment you can make is in yourself." Warren Buffet said that, so we should probably listen to him.

- Invest in people: Like Denzel Washington said, "At the end, it's not about what you have or even what you've accomplished. It's about who you've lifted up, who you've made better. It's about what you've given back."

- Invest in the environment: We all need to think about what kind of planet we're going to leave the generations after us.

- Donate: Drop off shelf-stable foods and essential items to your local food bank and charities.

- Shop local: Support local small businesses and your local economy. Just like author and educator, Anna Lappé says, "Every time you spend money, you're casting a vote for the kind of world you want."

- Get to know your neighbors: This may be outside your comfort zone, however, don't knock it until you've tried it! Even Bruce H. Lipton, American developmental biologist says, "Human beings are not meant to live alone. There's a fundamental biological imperative that propels you and every organism on this planet to be in a community, to be in relationship with other organisms."

- It's ok to take a break. "If you get tired, learn to rest, not to quit." said Banksy, a pseudonymous British street artist, political activist and film director.

- If you're feeling ambitious, organize your own fundraising event! Enlist the help of your friends and family—what a great reason to throw a party!

- And finally, "It does not matter how slowly you go, as long as you do not stop." Thanks, Confucius.

Philanthropists don't do it to feed their egos, they do it because they care about their fellow humans. They do it because they have the privilege to lighten the burden of others. They do it because their hearts hurt from the injustices of our world. Fred Rogers once said, "We live in a world in which we need to share responsibility. It's easy to say, 'It's not my child, not my community, not my world, not my problem.' Then there are those who see the need and respond. I consider those people my heroes." Wow, just wow.

We are all in this together, we all have fundamental human needs to be met. The Six Human Needs, according to uplift.love; originally introduced by Anthony Robbins, "1. Certainty: The need for safety, security, comfort, order, consistency, control. 2. Variety: The need for uncertainty, diversity, challenge, change, surprise, adventure. 3. Significance: The need for meaning, validation, feeling needed, honored, wanted, special. 4. Love and connection: The need for connection, communication, intimacy and shared love with others. 5. Growth: The need for physical, emotional, intellectual and spiritual development. 6. Contribution: The need to give, care, protect beyond ourselves, to serve others and the good of all.

I've been very inspired by everything Mackenzie Scott has done; but we can't all be her, Oprah, Serena Williams, or the Clooney's. What you can do is start now, start where you are, start with whatever you have—you just have to care. Lao Tzu said, "The journey of a thousand steps begins with one step." Come on, you can't disagree with an ancient philosopher! Especially not one whose name literally means "Old Master", who I wholeheartedly agree with. Something is better than nothing, friends. LET'S GO! See you on the other side!

CHAPTER 28
KINGMAKERS: THE MENTOR

"Do not try to be a king, instead, be a kingmaker. As a kingmaker, you will be more intelligent, astute, and able than kings; you will be admired by kings.

—Your friend, Shiv Verma

This chapter is dedicated to all the wise teachers, mentors and gurus of the world. Some say, "Think like a leader." I say, "Think like a mentor." A leader has the ability to make decisions and command others; a mentor has the ability to make many leaders. Leaders seek counsel and validation from their mentors; mentors seek to realize potential, to inspire, and to shape elite minds.

Guru's offer to train me was rooted in the potential that he recognized in me. He felt that I could've potential of becoming a successful trader in a decent time. He was right; if only I had learned the discipline and prioritized it—without getting carried away by mighty emotions. It's time to prove myself to both of my Gurus and life coaches, Guru and my sister. This also feels like my opportunity to pay it forward; to take the wisdom I acquired from them and share it with all of you. I genuinely hope to see you succeed in life.

There's this notion in the corporate world that being "#1" equals success. I must disagree. Brian Tracy best described it, "Successful people continually look for chances to assist others. Unsuccessful people frequently ask, "What's in it for me?" I wholeheartedly believe that our greatest victories in life often result from supporting others in their endeavors.

10 Traits of Positive People Who Have Fulfilling Lives:

1. Higher purpose: Positive humans aim to serve a purpose beyond themselves; when you ask what drives them, they talk about positively impacting others. Negative humans are often only concerned about their own goals; when you ask what drives them, their answers often lack the bigger picture.

2. Practice gratitude: Positive humans regularly practice gratitude; they know that their blessings are mostly due to privilege. Negative humans are self-absorbed; they often think they're superior to others.

3. Positive energy: Positive humans lift others up while negative humans tend to drag others down. Positive humans inspire others and make them feel good, while negative humans can be exhausting and make others feel bad.

4. Good listener: Positive humans hold space for others, make people feel seen and heard, don't interrupt or rush to give advice, and follow the speaker's lead. They ask follow-up questions to make sure they understand what was said and show genuine interest. Negative humans often listen to respond, are too opinionated, don't have a real sense of empathy, can be pretty arrogant and say a lot of "ME, ME, ME!"

5. Unselfish: Positive humans ask, "How can I make a difference?" Negative humans ask, "What's in it for me?"

6. Make people feel important = acknowledge their importance: Positive humans notice things about people, express their admiration for them, remember and use people's names, aim to connect on a deeper level, give others credit when credit is due, and value people's time. Negative humans could talk about themselves all day, rarely ask about others, have superficial friendships, and usually aren't there when people need them.

7. Firm values & beliefs: Those who lead a fulfilling life have powerful principles that they live by. Those who have an

unfulfilling life often show very little concern regarding whether their behavior is morally right or wrong.

8. Careful speaker: People who lead fulfilling lives know that their words can either make others feel better or worse—and make themselves feel better or worse. People who lead unfulfilling lives tend to complain a lot and put a negative spin on good things.

9. A healthy mind does not speak ill of others: We've all heard this quote, "Great minds discuss ideas; average minds discuss events; small minds discuss people." Believe it or not, according to Quote Investigator, there's no evidence that Eleanor Roosevelt or Socrates said this. However, QI did find, "The earliest strong match appeared in a 1901 autobiography by Charles Stewart. As a child in London, Stewart listened to the conversation of dinner guests such as history scholar Henry Thomas Buckle." Apparently, it was Buckle who said, "Men and women range themselves into three classes or orders of intelligence; you can tell the lowest class by their habit of always talking about persons; the next by the fact that their habit is always to converse about things; the highest by their preference for the discussion of ideas." After that, the quote evolved during decades of circulation and was misattributed to many individuals. So, if really smart people have been sharing this quote for over a century, I think it's safe to say that it's excellent advice.

10. Accountability: Accountable people are honest with themselves and others and can own up to their mistakes. They can set aside their pride and ask for help when needed. They don't play the blame game or make excuses for their faults. They're capable of self-reflection. Unaccountable people often struggle with low emotional intelligence. Many tend to blame others for their problems, make excuses for themselves, and aren't exactly team players. They may also have a victim mentality to dodge responsibility.

CHAPTER 29
TRADING REWIRED: LESS IS MORE

"Persistence guarantees that results are inevitable."

—Paramahansa Yogananda

Several times during my pursuit of day trading, I questioned myself if it was truly meant for me. As mentioned in Chapter 25: The Traits, this is a question we all should ask ourselves. Be honest and objective in your assessment.

Upon reflection, I knew that trading full-time was not for me. The idea of spending 8 hours each day buying and selling highly liquid stocks for profits sounds exhausting to me and—that's ok. There's no reason to knowingly put yourself in a position that you know will lead to burnout. We all need to learn to listen to our gut and body. This is why many traders who want to execute that many trades each day use trading bots (or automated software programs) that follow their defined rules of entries and exits.

Nowadays, I'm able to stay up-to-date with the market and my trading system daily, however, I don't trade daily. It felt good to release expectations—and find balance and self-assurance! Sometimes, I don't execute a trade for days, because the setup is not within my comfort zone. Other times, I trade multiple times a day by going with the flow.

Currently, I identify as a combination of an occasional day trader, frequent swing trader, and short to mid-term investor. My long-term investments are still being managed by my financial advisor and CPA, to avoid putting all my eggs in the same basket. Also, as a firm believer of mastering one skill at a time, instead of being a "Jack of all trades, master of none," I'd rather take my time becoming 100% confident in my long-term investing discipline.

This book has really become my newfound passion. I'd spend roughly 5-6 hours per week trading and 5-6 hours per week writing. After this book is published and released along with its audiobook (especially made for those of you who may prefer listening over reading), I'm hoping to compile a treasure trove of my experiences in the exciting metaverse (a.k.a. crypto). My goal is to continue hand-curating "trail guides" for all of you (with trail info, routes, maps, and detailed reviews) so you can avoid getting lost on this long-distance hike. "Why, Shiv?" You ask? Well, because "getting lost" not only entails extra miles and getting delayed, but could also mean injuries—minor, moderate, serious, or critical.

In the meantime, I'll continue with my day job, while gradually shifting my focus towards my ikigai; inadvertently inspired by my CEO's regular conference calls. My ikigai is to touch the lives of beings on this planet. I've already begun a small-scale operation to help fulfill my sister's philanthropic dream. Only time will tell—how much value and for how long—I'll be able to bring to the world.

If for some reason, you're still curious what my trading system looks like, please revisit Chapter 4: Surfers vs. Traders and Chapter 7: The Resurgent—where I went back to my basics. Truth be told, this book helped me immensely, after intentionally and thoroughly inspecting all aspects of my philosophy and approach. What started as a private journal to help me identify my shortcomings, has turned into a handbook containing the very essence of my trading discipline. Now, as a master sailor (a.k.a. thriving trader), I'll share my survival guide with you all, in anticipation of your transformation.

We as traders must endlessly remind ourselves that there are countless trading strategies out there—and not a single one can be 100% foolproof. Whenever you encounter someone claiming that they have "a sure-fire strategy" that's infallible, I suggest you run in the other direction. Save your precious time, energy, and money; because what makes a trading strategy work is to devise your trading system out of an unshakable trading discipline. As long as the market exists, this will hold true. Refer to Chapters 4 (surfers), Chapter 7 (the resurgent), Chapter 21 (the fisherman), and Chapter 22 (the sailor) as needed. "This is the way!"

This chapter was created to summarize and share some useful information related to common trading strategies out there; including valuable references. Gentle nudge: choose strategies that you're comfortable with; everyone is different, there's no "one size fits all" strategy. You may be surprised what you'll discover as you explore uncharted waters below!

Whatever you choose, just keep in mind that scaling in and out of your trades is an art that comes with pros (minimize risks and maximize profits) and cons (the risk of a trade reversing against you; the more positions you have open, the more you lose). Most importantly: (1) Your trading capital does not equal all of your savings; it should be 20% of your overall net worth, at the most. This lowers your chance of losing your shirt. (2) Only risk 1-2% or less of your trading capital on a single trade. (3) If you find yourself on a losing streak, STOP. It's time to re-evaluate your trades and yourself (follow the steps mentioned in Chapter 24: The Pro Gamer).

It may seem like a daunting task; the challenge of choosing and mastering a trading strategy that suits your financial goals and personality. A helpful exercise: Research the most prevalent day trading strategies today, narrow them down to 4 (or 5 at the most) that seem to align with you and your needs. After this, I'm pretty confident that you'll be able to choose one that's the best for you. If you already have a strategy, then you can instead evaluate it and journal all the pros and cons. This will help you diagnose and troubleshoot your methods so you can level up.

Helpful tip: Document and keep track of your trades, so you can easily review which ones were profitable and which ones were not. You can also regularly visit me at Rewired.Guru—and check for updates, new findings, and additional tips and tricks! I'm still working on figuring out a balance between how much advice I will routinely post on my website versus everything else that I do.

Before we jump into trading philosophy and top trading strategies: Please make sure to TAKE YOUR TIME when developing your trading strategy. Your trading style depends on what your personality is like and which chart time frame you choose (1, 5, 10, 15, 30, or 60 minutes). For example: if you're one of those people who can sit in front of their trading charts all day, entering and exiting trades every few seconds or minutes, then you may have some scalping potential. However, if you only want to trade part-time using a longer strategy that gives you more time to think things over, then swing-trading may be just the thing for you.

Trading philosophy: There isn't one cookie-cutter philosophy for all traders, instead, we each develop our own with our individual beliefs and principles. This consists of several elements such as risk management, trading strategies, trading expectations, risk tolerance, and individual capital status. Your SOP will be a combination of all of these elements. Next up, top trading strategies that can produce more successful results when utilized together with other technical analysis.

Trend trading: Buy when the price trends up and sell when the price trends down. Usually, trend traders will enter a long position when the price goes up and enter a short position when the price goes down. This strategy is widely used in all markets such as forex, crypto, and stocks.

Day trading: Enter trades, exit trades, and profit from small price movements, all on the same day. Day traders need to consider factors such as liquidity, volume, and volatility before opening a position (often using candlestick patterns, trend lines, and volume bars).

Scalping: Quickly profits from small price changes and frequently reselling. Scalpers usually have 1-5 minutes to determine their entry and exit strategies and make hundreds of trades per day; some use scalping bots that perform short (minutes to hours) trades for them.

Fibonacci retracements: One of the most common technical analysis tools; Fibonacci numbers are used to identify support and resistance levels, as well as predetermine stop loss and take profit targets before a trade. *According to Britannica: The Fibonacci sequence was noted by medieval Italian mathematician, Fibonacci (Leonardo Pisano), in his Liber Abaci (Book of the Abacus), which also popularized Hindu-Arabic numerals and the decimal number system in Europe. The sequence of numbers 1, 1, 2, 3, 5, 8, 13, 21 (and so on), each of which, after the second, is the sum of the two previous numbers"* Thankfully, traders can calculate the "38.2% Fibonacci ratio" and the "61.8% Fibonacci ratio" using their charting software.

Breakout trading: A type of momentum trading. When a price moves beyond one of these levels, it's called a breakout. Breakout traders use technical analysis to identify breakouts and enter trades where they predict the breakout will happen. Often, this means they have to be quick and aggressive. Many enjoy breakout trading because they know almost immediately how the trade will go.

Swing trading: This means that trades are made for both movements in any financial market. They buy when the market is going up and short when it's going down. They study technical analysis and trade in overbought and oversold situations. When there's a strong trend, swing traders look for retracements. *According to the Trading Setups Review, "Swing traders love retracements. When a trend retraces, it offers a potential low-risk/high-reward entry into the market. The 50% retracement trading strategy is great for patient swing traders: Wait for a powerful price thrust, then, wait for a nice 50% retracement. If you're afraid of missing the trend and are tempted to enter before price retraces to the 50% level, you cannot execute this strategy."*

Position trading: A popular strategy where traders hold a position for a long time (until a trend peaks), often months or years, disregarding small price fluctuations and focusing on profiting from long-term trends. Position traders tend to use fundamental analysis to identify the right entry and exit points and have a risk management plan, usually a stop-loss level.

Overbought and oversold trading: Often used in forex and the stock market, it identifies overbought and oversold levels at support and resistance levels through RSI (relative strength index). This belongs to a family of trading tools known as oscillators (which oscillate when the market moves). When the RSI is above 70%, the market is considered overbought. This means that traders are speculating that the market may return to a downtrend. Similarly, when the RSI goes below 30, it's speculated that the market may enter an up movement again.

News trading: Primarily relies on opportunities based on market news and expectations. As opposed to textbook technical analysis, news traders focus on signals generated in the market by "trigger events". This is a tricky one because price reactions to news events can be very short-lived, which can leave traders in undesirable positions.

My Trading Mantra:

"Buy the rumor, sell the news!" —An Old Wall Street Adage

(According to the Balance, "In this strategy, you buy a security based on speculation about an upcoming news event and you sell the security when that

news is announced. Disadvantages of the strategy include lack of accuracy and potential loss of opportunity on decisions not made quickly enough.")

End-of-day trading: These trades are entered when the market is scheduled to close, with the understanding that the price will settle at the end of the day. Usually, they look at the closing price and price movement from the previous day to decide if they will enter a long position (meaning they will profit if the stock rises) or a short position (meaning they will profit if the stock falls).

Trading micro E-mini futures: This allows you to take positions on the big four U.S. indexes for a tenth of the price of regular contracts. Occasionally, I'll use this strategy, set up my trade with predetermined levels (of buy, sell, and stop loss), and set my buy price at what one would normally set as their stop loss point. This tactic works surprisingly well, turning most of these trades into profits. I'll share more about this in the near future on Rewired.Guru after I make more observations, analyze the results and present my findings.

And there you have it! I wish you the best of luck with testing new trading techniques (or improving your existing trading strategy) and building your very own trading plan. Before we move on to the Trading Anthem, an exercise to practice perspective: Have you ever watched ducks swim? They make it look so effortless; yet underwater, they are paddling VIGOROUSLY. So, if you think "some traders look like they're just gracefully gliding along," remember that underneath the surface, they're operating on a trading discipline that has been with them through thick and thin! The truth is, they've achieved Trading Rewired, which allows them to make it look easy.

BONUS: MY TRADING ANTHEM

"When we repeatedly bring certain types of feelings to our mind, they develop into an attitude. And that attitude, when it hardens and becomes natural to our personality, develops into a mindset."

—Swami Mukundananda

Every single day that you decide to trade, read these lyrics or listen to this song. Heck, sing it to yourself in the shower if you'd prefer that! I'm not kidding. The most effective way to become fluent in another language is to listen to it, speak it, and read it on a daily basis. Akin to putting your hand over your heart to pledge your allegiance for your trading discipline and system. According to Forex.in.rs, 95% of traders lose money, based on Contentworks research and forex trading statistics. It's time for your trading to get rewired so you don't become a statistic!

Whether you listen to it while you're pumping iron at the gym, out on a brisk walk, or simply dancing it out in your kitchen; According to iSpring Solutions, "German psychologist Hermann Ebbinghaus, who is known for his discovery of the so-called Forgetting Curve. He explored the exponential nature of forgetting. Research shows that an average learner forgets 70% of what they learned within 24 hours and 90% of what they learned in a week if they don't make an effort to retain it." Thankfully, they also found that blended learning styles, a mix of content types, microlearning, and practicing memory retrieval, can greatly improve knowledge retention. So, feel free to get creative with this!

"Get ready for the trading anthem

Say hello to Papa Shiv,

say hello to Papa Bull, say hello to Papa Bear

Every day, in every way, I get better and better, everywhere

I will follow my trades in disciplined ways

"This is the way!"

I'm never greedy, nor do I grieve in my trades

I never miss on my stop losses, nor miss taking the profits

I never borrow in my trades,

nor ever sorrowing over faltered grades

I will never risk high, nor shall I miss the ride

This is the way; this is the way!

I believe in me, I believe in me, my Trading Rewired

I believe in you, I believe in you, says Papa Shiv

Every day I learn, every day I grow

I follow my entry plan, I stick to my exit clan

I value my trading, I protect capital

I surf the wave, I ride the pave

I shall not falter, I shall prevail

I am consistent, I am consistent, I sing my trading anthem

I believe in you, I believe in you, says Papa Shiv

I profit high, risk low

I care for my health, I value my life

My family comes first, my health is wealth

"This is the way! This is the way!"

I ride the bull, I slide the bear

I am patient when markets tear

I rise, I learn, I have no fear

I'm the noble giver; I'm the wiser; dreamer

I believe in me, believe in me, my Trading Rewired

I believe in you, I believe in you, my trading anthem

This is the way!"

Inspired by my mom's words of wisdom that she used to say to me nearly every day. Her entire life's worth of wisdom, accumulated, and spoken into existence for me. This is why I created this anthem, so I can do the same for you. My hope is that you will listen to this regularly during your first month of trading. You can also watch or listen to this original trading anthem at Rewired.Guru, Spotify, YouTube, and more. If you create your own anthem, please share it with the Rewired community and I via the connect section of Rewired.Guru!

PUT YOUR TRADING PANTS ON: SELF-INVENTORY

This is the crème de la crème, my friends. Revisit this questionnaire once a month to compare your answers and progress. Feel free to use them as prompts for your personal journal. *Visit Rewired.Guru for updated self-inventory questionnaires and recommendations tailored to your answers.*

1. What are three daily habits I need to develop that will enhance my self-awareness?

   ____
   ____
   ____
   ____
   ____

2. What are three daily habits I need to develop that will strengthen my trading discipline?

   ____
   ____
   ____
   ____
   ____

3. What are five things I am grateful for?

   ____
   ____
   ____
   ____
   ____

4. How will I take care of my physical health?

   ____
   ____
   ____

5. How will I take care of my mental health?

6. How will I become or remain accountable?

7. What does my self-talk sound like (both in life and while trading)?

8. If my self-talk is mean, frustrated, or defeated, how will I unlearn it and replace it with positive, (market) strategy-focused talk?

9. What can I work on while the market is closed?

10. How will I commit to a trade review journal so I can identify what I'm doing right and wrong each day? What questions should I ask myself?

11. What will I do if I notice a few days where I lacked proper risk management (to avoid current trading losses snowballing into even larger trading losses)?

12. Am I the type of person that can become stubborn in positions, turning small losses into large ones? If so, how will I remedy this?

13. Am I having fun trading, even though it's hard work?

____

____

____

____

____

14. Am I able to resist temptation; especially when I feel "bored" and crave excitement (a.k.a. an adrenaline rush)? How?

____

____

____

____

____

15. Will I be able to ask myself these key questions before executing every single trade?

- What is the sentiment in this stock?
- What indicators do I see?
- Where do I expect this move to go?
- Is this just scalping or a "big picture" trade?
- How are the securities on my watch list doing?
- What entry and exit point should I choose and why?
- Where should I add to the position and why?
- Should I not add to this position?
- What indicators and decisions have gone well for me in the past? Which ones ended poorly?

- What did I tell myself I need to watch out for?

16. How will I ensure that I stick to my trading plan and consistently journal my trade reviews?

17. How will I pay it forward?

Epilogue

As I'm finalizing this book, preparing for publication, and making arrangements for the production of this audiobook, I've experienced a 10-day lull in trading. 10 days of underwhelming profits for the author of this book; the timing could not be worse—or better? Upon reflection of the 10 days of disappointing trades, I saw that on half of those days, I didn't take certain trades because I couldn't find trading indicators (that I was comfortable with for my setup). One of the days, I missed my chance to enter a good trade when my setup was there, because I wasn't available. On the remaining days, I got antsy and started to force trades.

Even after writing an entire book about following your trading system and endlessly preaching the importance of your trading discipline, I got diverted. Thankfully, I was firm with my entry and exit points, so on this 11th day, I'm sitting at 0 profit 0 loss. Of course I'm not happy about this. Of course I'm a little disappointed in myself. So why am I adding this to the book and sharing this with you? The answer is simple, because we are human, because no matter how disciplined we are, we still have emotions—and that's ok.

As you know, from reading about my journey to this point, just two years ago, this could have gone very differently. After 10-days of disappointment, I could've spiraled, crashed and burned. However, here I am, after finally pausing—amidst the busyness of life and conducted "trade triage"; I assessed casualties, determined the cause of injuries, and performed damage control. This is all I can hope for you, my friend.

Also, I gave myself a little break, took my car out for a long scenic drive, ran some errands, went on a nice long walk, and jogged. I even danced around my house, enjoyed a nice long hot shower, meditated, and brainstormed out loud. It's almost the 5th day of my break from trading and I'm thrilled I took this time to wrap up this book and get all my ducks in a row. As I was out jogging, I remembered that trading is a marathon, not a race, sometimes you need to slow down and catch your breath. Also, training for a marathon requires patience in yourself and the process. We need to trust ourselves and the journey.

Whoever says that "there's no such thing as trading part-time" is lying to you and themselves. Trading is a passion of mine that takes up roughly 4.17% of my day; while generating the most satisfying results for me. The remaining 95.83% of my day is for myself, the day job that I enjoy, my family, my hobbies, and paying it forward. I hope you remember this too. Turn the page for my letter to you.

An open letter to you, my friend:

Bulls and bears are bigger, stronger, and far more powerful than we are. Why become a bull-fighter or bear-fighter when you can be the ringmaster? Equip yourself with a combination of knowledge, skills, and repetition that'll allow you to recognize their talent—instead of giving them a reason to launch a lethal attack on you.

Thank you for spending your valuable time with me; listening to my story and reading my experiences. I am truly humbled! Remember, trading is not for everyone. Every success has an invisible motivation, drive, and a passion that fuels the entire marathon! All that matters is that you make the most out of your time, because you're only young once! Hey, 50 or 60 is still young too!

May you be blessed with good health, joy, love, and all the benefits life has to offer. May you never stop touching people's hearts with your positivity and kindness. I hope to see you at my website: "Rewired.Guru"! Keep your eyes peeled for my next book, a guide to becoming crypto-literate; to help you navigate the metaverse! *"Until our paths cross." -Cara Dune (The Mandalorian)*

Wishing you all the best,

Your friend, **Shiv Verma**

Made in United States
Troutdale, OR
11/03/2026

56844376R10111